THE CLASSIC
Ferrari

THE CLASSIC
Ferrari

GODFREY EATON

First Published in 1983 by
Bison Books Corp.
17 Sherwood Place
Greenwich, CT 06830
U.S.A.

ISBN 0 86124 108 8

Printed in Hong Kong

Page 2 and 3: Alberto Ascari's 1952 Tipo 500.
Below: The exceptionally elegant Daytona Spyder.

Contents

The prancing horse

The 750 Monza seen here was a large-capacity development of the four-cylinder, 2.5-liter sportscar first seen at Monza in 1953, and the bigger versions began to appear over the following years until the 860 in late 1955.

For three and a half decades the black prancing horse emblem has imprinted the name Ferrari in the minds of those people whose interest in automobiles goes beyond their more mundane use as a means of transportation. It is not difficult to understand why, for Ferrari stands for engine power, for high speed touring and for haut-monde styling. So where does all this fit in with a man who emerged from World War I in poor health with only a scrap of paper given to him by his commanding officer as an introduction to the giant FIAT enterprise for a job which, in any case, they denied him?

Enzo Ferrari had no formal engineering education (he had refused to go to a technical college), but he did have a practical introduction as his father owned a metal and motor business. So even if in his earlier years he had been unable to read a draughtsman's design from the drawing board, he probably knew as much about the mechanics of a car as any trained automobile engineer.

It is said that, as a young man, Enzo Ferrari had two ambitions. To become a singer (which he was unlikely to achieve, being tone deaf) and to be a journalist. This latter career he has partially fulfilled for, from the time he formed his Scuderia Ferrari in 1929, he would issue yearly 'bulletins' and subsequently annual publications on his organization's progress. And from the time he set up his own factory, in 1946, to build racing and gran turismo cars he held an annual press conference which was attended by all the leading motoring journalists. Ferrari has a keen sense of the press which has not always been kind to him but then he has always been a man to pursue his own course.

The young Enzo's father would take him to the local circuits whenever a race meeting was held and there can be little doubt that on these occasions the speed, the smell and the dust and danger must surely have fired his enthusiasm and ambition to be not only a racing driver but to plan his future life to become the foremost name in automobile history.

After working with two relatively minor concerns in the motor industry Ferrari's arrival at the Portobello firm of Alfa Romeo in 1920 was his first major step up the hard road towards his ultimate goal. For a while he formed part of the racing team with two great drivers, Antonio Ascari and Giuseppe Campari, but it was as a co-ordinator and welder of an organization that the company found him most useful.

While the racing of cars was far from being a cheap method of keeping a company's name in the forefront it was at the time one of the most effective. To this end Alfa Romeo set up a separate department, to which Ferrari was assigned, with the sole object of becoming a major contender for grand prix honours.

Ferrari had already persuaded Luigi Bazzi to leave FIAT which was an astute move, as Bazzi not only remained a close friend and associate of Ferrari during his lifetime but he was to become one of the world's greatest technical engineers sorting out the myriad problems which inevitably arise when a new design takes to the circuits. But Alfa still needed a designer for their grand prix car, as the P1 had been abandoned when Ugo Sivocci had been fatally injured during practice for the 1923 Italian Grand Prix at Monza. Whether

Below: The 250 LMB, one version of the most successful range of Ferrari sports racing cars. Inset: The same model, but a different car and a different viewpoint.

it was Ferrari who persuaded Vittorio Jano to leave FIAT or the Alfa Romeo board is irrelevant but there can be little doubt that Ferrari was in the background showing that he was already a man who could pick a particular individual for a particular project. This was an invaluable trait which he has never lost.

Ever the opportunist, Ferrari discussed his plans to form his own racing team with two young and wealthy industrialists at an important dinner function. The outcome was the formation in December 1929 of Scuderia Ferrari. The basic idea was to race the Alfa Romeo cars (mainly the sports racing cars) using amateur drivers who would share in any prize money going but would not require professional fees. He was astute enough, however, to hire one professional driver which would give status to his team and would also ensure that race promoters would pay start money. It didn't take Ferrari long to realize that amateur drivers did not bring the prestige and money necessary to run a racing team so he disposed of them. A lot of things went right during the thirties particularly during the first few years when the competition was not all that strong but things started to go sour with the advent of the two German teams, Mercedes and Auto Union, which had almost unlimited resources. On the other hand Alfa Romeo was pressed for money and while new cars were in evidence their development was undoubtedly restricted. The Scuderia was not without its successes in the major grand prix but it had to rely mainly on income from the less prestigious events. Both Ferrari and Luigi Bazzi became disenchanted and even went so far as to

build the two Bi-Motores in 1935 which although highly successful in formula libra were ineligible for the major grand prix. Ferrari had little or no say in what cars should be produced which must have been more than annoying but he was permitted to build a team of 1500cc straight-eight cars for voiturette racing, the Alfettas, and was loaned Gioacchino Colombo as consultant.

A further blow came in 1938 when the Alfa Romeo board decided to race their cars, forming Alfa Corse. They invited Ferrari to head the team but as he was in constant conflict with the chief engineer, a Spaniard, Wilfredo Ricart, he quit.

Under the severance terms Ferrari was forbidden to build any cars carrying his own name for a period of four years. Also the Scuderia could not operate for the same period so in the meantime Ferrari set up a new firm, Auto-Avio Construzioni.

It is difficult, once more, to speculate on what Ferrari might have done had not World War II intervened. He was certainly not idle, being a man of activity, and his first venture was to construct, with the help of his 'team' and some outside assistance, two 1500cc eight-in-line sports racing cars. Called 815 Vettura the idea was to enter them for the 1940 Mille Miglia. The construction was based on FIAT parts as that company was offering financial inducements to constructors who used their parts and were successful. The cars did not bear the name Ferrari and he was careful to point out that they had been built for customers.

Ferrari couldn't have had much money at that time but he was building up a business which took off as a result of lucrative contracts manufacturing parts for the war effort. In fact business prospered, enabling him to build much larger premises. In 1946 his new factory which, although it had received bomb damage, was usable, he had a strong workforce, including an invaluable nucleus who knew about racing cars, and most important he knew what he wanted and where he was going. Although the first objective was to build a team of grand prix cars their initial appearance was delayed until the Italian Grand Prix on 5 September 1948 held over the Valentino Park circuit at Turin. In the meantime three *competizione* or sports racing cars were available by 1947 designated 125 C or 125 S.

While the same basic engine was used for the grand prix and sports racing cars it was not long before there were variations. It is also of note that Colombo's 60 degree V12 unit was the basis of a number of engines, including gran turismo units, right up to 1970–71 when the 5-liter V12 powered the 512 S and M sports racing cars.

Colombo didn't remain long as chief engineer and consultant, as his number two, Aurelio Lampredi had his own ideas which, while not acceptable to Colombo, found favour with Ferrari. One thing Ferrari must have wanted almost more than anything else at that stage of his career – to defeat the almost invincible Alfa Romeo 1500cc supercharged straight eight racing cars. He achieved his objective, not by winning the 1952 formula 1 championship which he narrowly lost, but because Alfa Romeo were in no position to build a new grand prix car and further development of the type 159 was not feasible. Ferrari's 375 Fl unsupercharged 4.5-liter car designed by Lampredi would be top dog. It was unfortunate that the 375 Fl had no 'takers' so formula 1 racing waned until it was revived in 1954.

Apart from formula 1 racing Ferrari was interested and totally involved in sports car, prototype and gran turismo racing which, at times, meant he overstretched his resources to the detriment of the cars. This can be noted in a number of tipos which had they been developed further could have become 'winners'. All that can be said is that Ferrari knows his business and what he wants, and lesser mortals should keep their views to themselves!

In his 80th year Ferrari decided to change direction and abandoning the the flat 12 racing cars produced his 1500cc V6 turbo charged formula 1 car for the 1981 season. Not many men of his age would have bothered to take a new line and although it is said that his enthusiasm for racing has waned it must give him great satisfaction to see how well his 'new baby' is doing. Even those motor racing individuals who may not be Ferrari orientated must surely pay tribute to a man who has always upheld the sport of motor racing and who has contributed so much toward its progress and continuance.

It is always difficult to look into the future whether it be forecasting the shape or the power pack of the automobile. Apart from current Ferrari formula 1 cars, which use a turbocharger to get extra power from the boost, will the road cars change direction and go the same way? Indications at present say no, for the V8s (the 308 and Mondial) have been worked over and have come up with four valve heads per cylinder with the other necessary equipment which four valve heads require – such as revised camshafts, new pistons and new metals. This, however, does not mean that Ferrari or Fiat are in any way anti-turbo for road cars as the 208 which has been around in Italy for some time now has a turbocharger. In May 1982 at the Turin show the 2-liter car was shown as the 208 GTB and GTS. They were KKK-boosted with a quoted output of 220bhp at 7000rpm which was greater than the 214bhp of the 308 GTBi.

Most of the turbocharged Ferraris have been prepared either by private owners or specialists in the field of turbocharging as there are quite a number of firms producing the necessary equipment. Some may question the point of boosting the power of any car which is already powerful. But in the USA where there are strict emission and other laws the relatively heavy Ferraris are at a disadvantage to other lighter and very much cheaper automobiles. Frequently outaccelerated, the Ferrari owner with his expensive sports-type car feels disgruntled and so resorts to the somewhat expensive ploy of adding a turbocharger.

At the present time there are two main suppliers of the necessary hardware in the States – BAE and Ameritech – and one in England – Janspeed. BAE has sold nearly 300 conversion kits to Ferrari owners. With a boost of 5.5psi on the 308 the bhp goes from 214 to 245 and it has been said that using 108 octane fuel and a 9psi boost up to 300bhp has been available at the rear wheels!

A privately owned 512 BB turbocharged by BAE, with revised fuel injection system and with a 10psi boost is alleged to have a power output of 600bhp and when the engine has been wound up to 7800rpm in 5th gear the maximum speed is around 200mph.

The Ameritech system conversions are said to produce a figure in excess of those obtained by BAE. The Janspeed system using the Garrett blower at 5.5psi can increase the bhp by between 30–40.

Few conversions have been carried out in Europe but the Carma FF 308 GTB4 Biturbo is one example. Unfortunately this prototype car flattered to deceive on the circuits. Tremendous power, acceleration and speed but reliability was virtually nil and the car never finished a race. The power output was almost ridiculous – for qualifying the boost was turned up to produce between 830 and 840bhp but on race days this is reduced to a mere 750bhp!

For those who want a ready to run turbo Ferrari in Europe it is necessary to go to West Germany where the enterprising Willy Koenig can supply the 308 series, including the Mondial 8, fully equipped. The power output of the 308 GTB/GTS being 305bhp and that of the Mondial 8 is 280bhp.

However, of greater interest to the Ferrarist is the news that in April 1982 Ferrari announced a 308 sports car to be built as a limited production – a figure of 200 has been quoted. The engine is placed longitudinally at the rear which is quite a departure. Will this be a four valve fuel injection turbocharged car? Whatever it is, it will be welcome news that a real sports car will once again carry the prancing horse logo. Reputed output is up to 700bhp and bearing in mind the boost of the Carma FF this is not beyond the realms of probability.

On an entirely different tack and into the highest up-market bracket there will, in the not too distant future, emerge the ultimate luxury Ferrari. For the present the model, which was first shown in prototype form, over two years ago, is known as the 'Ferrari-Pinin'. A four door, four seater limousine, it is to be powered by the boxer flat 12 unit as used in the current 512 BBi. The engine, however, will be front-mounted. The driver's compartment is, if the illustrations and brochure are to be believed, full of electronic gadgetry which will keep the driver busy enough on checking out whether all is well. Presumably he will have time now and again to look up to see where he is going!

There can be little doubt that the Ferrari-Fiat organization are going all-out to capture what they might consider as their share of the Rolls-Royce market but with a car whose styling is far more appealing than that of the R-R.

Perhaps a limousine of this nature will not have a great appeal to many Ferrarists thinking that such an automobile should be driven by a liveried chauffeur. But those owners of the 400 series will, no doubt, be delighted to know that an even more up-market Ferrari is on the way!

All else apart the styling for such a car, if the present illustrations are anything to go by, is in keeping with the status it will achieve. Rounded with a hint of voluptuousness and set off by a grille which denotes that certain Ferrari aggression.

At one time Ferrari the man decided what should or should not be built, setting markets which other designers and manufacturers had to follow if they wished to compete. Now it is the marketing men and accountants who decide what the requirements are. The world moves on but is it for the better when there are so many look-alike cars on the roads of the world? Perhaps we should take a look now and again under the hood or rear deck to identify the car.

Right: The 250 Testa Rossa prototype in action, complete with damaged front end.

Below right: 250LM at the Nurburgring 1000.
Below: Il Commendatore, Enzo Ferrari.

One of the prettiest Dinos ever made, fifteen of these 2-liter V6 cars were built and raced by the factory in endurance and hillclimbs with some success in 1966 and 1967

Sports and sports racers

In simple terms the dictionary will reveal that the word prototype means 'the first or original type or model from which anything is copied'. However, the interpretation of prototype in this chapter refers to cars built for a specific purpose to conform to regulations for sports racing championship events as laid down by the authorities controlling motor sport. Such cars were manufactured for speed and for endurance races on closed circuits and designed supposedly as a basis for future production models. This being the case there were two places in the cockpit and a certain amount of equipment which would be necessary should they ever be driven on the open road, all of which was somewhat non-sensical.

While Ferrari had over the years built one-off prototypes, entering them for events for which they would be eligible prior to going into limited production runs, it was not until 1961/62 that he became heavily committed to gran turismo and sports car prototypes. At that time British constructors had proved conclusively to the racing fraternity that the logical position for the power plant was behind the driver. Now, while Ferrari had shown that he could be flexible and seemingly, without effort, could produce new engines and cars almost at will, he was not totally convinced that the day of the front-engined racing and sports racing car was over, any more than he was convinced that the disk brake was more efficient than the drum brake.

So 1961/62 was to be a turning point with a number of rear or mid-mounted prototypes coming from the factory which were the forerunners not only of the racing cars but more importantly of the sports racing cars, which carried the logo of the prancing horse to many championship victories.

The SP Cars

The SPs (Sports Prototypes) were a small but highly important series of V6 and V8 mid-engined cars evolved and developed by Maranello for sports car racing. Their beginnings are traced back to the regulations set out by the CSI for the new formula 2 racing to become effective in 1957. These stipulated displacement of up to 1500cc unsupercharged with pump fuel to be used in the first year and the higher octane aviation fuel from 1958. There was every prospect of Ferrari participation bearing in mind the highly successful seasons when the 166 F2 and 500 F2 cars reigned supreme.

Ferrari decided on a V6 layout for the new formula and the first car appeared at the Naples Grand Prix on 28 April 1957 where, running out of its class, Luigi Musso placed it third behind the two formula 1 Lancia-Ferraris of Mike Hawthorn and Peter Collins.

Ferrari's son Dino was prominent in the early discussions which influenced Ferrari in adopting the V6 layout and his name became associated with the cars using this engine configuration. His name also prefixed the V8 sports racing cars and continued to be used for the first mid-engined transverse mounted V8 gran turismo car of 1973, the 308 GT4 2+2, but his name was 'dropped' from the series in 1976 when the name and all badges were changed to Ferrari.

There have been three series of V6 engines used to power a range of formula 1, formula 2, sports racing and gran turismo cars. Vittorio Jano, the brilliant automobile engineer, who joined Ferrari in 1955, when he 'came over' with the Lancia racing department, was responsible for the first two series and Franco Rocchi, the third.

Jano's first effort was the formula 2 V6 engine of 1956/57 which was considered too advanced and complicated for private entrants so in 1959 a second simpler series was introduced.

The third design by Rocchi, in 1965, was also produced for formula 2 racing and at the same time Ferrari was looking for a unit to power a road-going car as the regulations for the formula stipulated that a minimum of 500 had to be built. Franco Rocchi decided to go back to Jano's 1957 design and this was to be one of the most successful designs to come from the factory, as in a variety of displacements it powered the front-engined Fiat Dinos which provided the necessary production basis for the formula 2 cars, a range of mid-engined sports racing prototypes and the mid-engined Dino 206 GT, Dino 246 GT and GTS road cars.

At his pre-season annual press conference on 13 February 1961, Ferrari unveiled two new cars, the mid-engined Dino 156 1500cc formula 1 contender and his prototype replacement for the 250 Testa Rossa series which had served him well in the sports racing championships – the Dino 246 SP mid-engined sports racing car. For both cars designer and engineer Chiti had adapted the Jano 1956/57 Dino engine derived from the 2.5-liter formula 1 cars.

Body styling was entirely new for a Ferrari and whilst not as attractive as the Testa Rossa had a purposeful look which meant business. The design had been evolved after Chiti had persuaded Ferrari to install a wind-tunnel. It was high-tailed from the back of the cockpit with a headrest fairing which ended in a sharp-edged form at the Kamm-type tail. The body design had a shortish nose and incorporated twin-

Right: The V6 Dino, showing the arrangement of the three 2bbl Webers.

nostrils which had been copied from a design by Fantuzzi.

Before the Sebring 12-hour race Richie Ginther was given the job of testing the works sports racing cars and found that the high rear deck was causing instability. Ginther, who had connections with the aircraft industry, solved the problem after trial and error by having a type of spoiler tacked to the lip of the car's tail. This cured the poor handling but at the same time dropped the car's speed.

A second car was ready in time for the Targa Florio run on 30 April over the Madonie circuit. Von Trips and Ginther drove the Sebring car while Phil Hill and Gendebien had the new one. Phil Hill, trying to make up time after a start line fiasco involving his co-driver, did considerable damage to the front end of his car. However, von Trips retrieved the day for Ferrari by taking his car first over the line and he also set a new lap record of 67.01mph.

For the Le Mans 24-hour race on 10–11 June the factory entered only one Dino 246 SP for Ginther and von Trips but von Trips ran out of fuel on the Mulsanne straight — a bad pit blunder! All was not lost for Maranello as the Phil Hill/Gendebien combination won in the TR1/61 (V12 Testa Rossa) and gave the Scuderia its seventh World Championship Sports Car title.

There was trauma at the factory during the winter of 1961 when a major row broke out with Romolo Tavoni (team manager), Carlo Chiti (chief engineer) and other highly placed personnel walking out. While Ferrari might have been distressed up to a point it has always been widely known that to him machines were of greater importance than men and there were others to take the place of those who left. True that development work was interrupted but Chiti had not been idle before his departure and Ferrari still had something to show at his 1962 press conference on 24 February. There were three new mid-engined sports racing cars on view, all of which looked alike externally, so it was just as well that the factory had taken the trouble to paint on each its type number. They were all Dinos and the smallest capacity car was the under 2-liter 196 SP introduced originally in 1958 as a customer 196 S sports racing car with a V6 engine. This engine was carried on in the 196 SP but with an increase in power to 210bhp at 7500rpm and a 5-speed transmission. Also in the line-up was the new Dino 286 SP with a swept volume of 2862cc. The engine was based on the original Chiti 60 degree 'half-V12' block. The compression ratio was 9.5:1 and the unit produced 260bhp at 6800rpm. Perhaps of greater interest to those present were two Dino 248 SPs developed by Chiti with 90 degree V8 units and with a displacement of 2458.7cc. The engine could be readily enlarged using a new crankshaft which increased the displacement to 2644.9cc and in this larger form the Dino 268 SP was rated at more than 260bhp at 7500rpm. All of these Dinos were sufficiently 'simple' to be sold to various teams who would find no difficulty in maintaining them. For 1961 the FIA had decreed a minimum height for windshields which displeased both constructors and drivers but this somewhat arbitary rule was dropped for 1962 and the rear decks of the new Dino SPs were lowered giving each car a far more handsome appearance.

The Daytona Speedway saw the first major sports car race for the 1962 season on 11 February. Two Ferraris appeared for the 3-hour race with Phil Hill partnering Ricardo Rodriguez in a revised-bodied 246 SP which was entered by Ricardo's father, while Luigi Chinetti's NART entered a 246 S for Buck Fulp who also shared his car with Rodriguez. Although Hill had set the pace a slow driver change-over cost him the race in which he finished second to Dan Gurney in a sick Lotus 19. Fulp was eighth.

After Hill and Gendebien had taken first place at Nurburgring in a 246 SP the 196 SP was given a new role and was handed over to Scuderia Sant' Ambroeus for Ludovico Scarfiotti to drive in the European Mountain Championship with Dragoni supervising. Generally speaking the event had been a preserve of the Porsches which was to be shattered in 1962. The 196 SP missed the first round but ran at the Fornovo-Monte Cassio climb on 10 June establishing a new record and beating four Porsches. A week later at Mont Ventoux the Porsche factory entered a 2-liter flat 8 spyder but it made no difference as the 196 SP smashed Maurice Trintignant's 1960 record by the huge margin of 24 seconds for the 13.4 mile climb. 8 July saw the 'circus' gather for the 10.75 mile climb at Trento-Bondone but once again Scarfiotti took the honours and on the resurfaced road collected a new record, reducing the time by an incredible 45 seconds. Scarfiotti

blew off the Porsches again on 22 July when the 196 SP set another hill climb record and the aggregate of the two runs bettered the closest Porsche by a fraction over 10 seconds. The unexpected happened at Ollon-Villars on 25 August when Scarfiotti was 0.2 seconds behind Sepp Greger's RS 1700 after two runs, no doubt due to running on two new and unscrubbed front tyres. This event clinched the title for Scarfiotti and the 196 SP so it was decided to forgo the final event.

Le Mans, to be run on 23–24 June showed a great diversification of cars entered by works and privateers. There were 15 Ferraris including 250 TR, 250 GT special, 250 short wheelbase, 250 GTO and GTO special. The works cars consisted of the surviving 268 SP for Baghetti/Scarfiotti, a 246 SP for the Rodriguez brothers while Mike Parkes and co-driver Bandini had a 330 LM berlinetta. The 268 SP had been running well when gearbox problems caused its retirement in the 18th hour. Meanwhile the Rodriguez brothers had been swapping the lead with Hill and Gendebien for 12 hours but were also sidelined with transmission troubles. Despite these set-backs Hill and Gendebien continued on their way to take first overall. Their car was designated by the works as 330TR/LM and powered by the 4-liter V12 400 Superamerica engine. It was a spyder and also sported the full rear deck width airfoil section behind the driver. These sections were known affectionately as 'basket handles'!

An interesting development and the whole purpose of the

'SP exercise' came together late in 1962 when a V12 unit was slipped into a 246 SP chassis. The car was tested at Modena and Monza with John Surtees at the wheel. The new concept certainly made its mark as Surtees proceeded to break Ginther's Monza lap record.

The 250 P

The car with which John Surtees broke Ritchie Ginther's lap record at Monza in November 1962 was the development model for the 250 P which Ferrari had on show at his press conference in March 1963. The original chassis was from a 246 SP but it had been 'stretched' to accommodate a V12 250 Testa Rossa engine – virtually the 3-liter unit with six 38 DCN Weber carburetors and dry sump lubrication. It was taken to the 1963 Targa Florio as a 'training' car but after a fuel line breakage it was severely damaged by fire.

The single overhead camshaft 3-liter V12 was rated at 300bhp at 7800rpm with six Weber carburetors and a compression ratio of 9.8:1.

Suspension was independent all round using double wishbones and concentric shock absorbers with coil springs. The disk brakes were placed inboard at the rear on either side of the transaxle assembly.

Under the hood could be found the oil tank for the dry sump lubrication, a radiator for oil cooling and the water radiator. The spyder bodywork was styled by Pininfarina and the Chiti nose, as seen on the SP series, was abandoned but the 'basket-handle' retained. The whole was compact and businesslike.

The 250 P contested the Sebring 12-hour on 23 March 1963 when two cars were entered. John Surtees, having his first race for the Scuderia, partnered by Lodovico Scarfiotti, placed their car first having covered some 209 laps. Second home was the other 250 P driven by Willy Mairesse and Nino Vaccarella. Third place was also filled by a Ferrari – the 1962 Le Mans winning car, the NART TR/61, handled by Graham Hill and Pedro Rodriguez and the next three cars home were 250 GTOs which also took 13th, 14th and 18th places. Quite a triumph for Ferrari, only to be topped in April, during the Le Mans trials, when Surtees lapped the circuit at 133mph clipping no less than 11.6 seconds from the lap record.

While the 250 P had only won two out of the three races so far contested there can be no doubt that Ferraris were on the crest of a wave and demonstrated their superiority once again during the 24-hour Le Mans endurance race on 15–16 June. The cars entered by the Scuderia were a mixed but interesting collection and there can be little doubt that Enzo Ferrari was determined to make every effort to win his fourth Le Mans race in a row. The 250 Ps were in the hands of Surtees/Mairesse, Mike Parkes/Maglioli and Scarfiotti/Bandini. There were four 330 LMs for the Americans Dan Gurney/Jim Hall, the Englishmen Jack Sears/Mike Salmon and the Frenchmen Noblet/Guichet while Masten Gregory and David Piper had a similar 3-liter car. Beurlys and Langlois had the fast, reliable 250 GTO as did Elde/Dumay.

Scarfiotti and Bandini won at an average speed of 118.5mph with the 250 GTO taking second overall and first in the GT class at 112.5mph. Following the GTO was another 250 P (Parkes/Maglioli) with the second GTO fourth. To round off this astounding parade of Ferraris the 330 LM of Sears/Salmon was fifth and the 3-liter berlinetta handled by Gregory and Piper sixth.

The 250 Ps had not finished their season as Pedro Rodriguez drove the NART car into second place at the Bridgehampton Double 500 on 15 September and followed this up a week later for the Canadian Grand Prix for sports cars held at Mosport which he won. Early December was 'cocktail time' at the Nassau Speed Week but Rodriguez once again acquitted himself quite well by coming in second in the Nassau Trophy and also the Governor's Cup, making 1963 a year to be remembered as the first rear engined V12s showed their tails to most of the competitors. The 250 P was Ferrari's venture into the rear engined V12 cars which he had every intention of marketing as gran turismos.

The 250 LM

Introduced at the Paris Salon in October 1963 the 250 berlinetta Le Mans was to all intents a 250 P with a roof, a vertical rear window with sail panels which tapered into the rear deck, and an air slot at the back in an effort to reduce any turbulence at the cut-off. Ferrari had intended the car as the gran turismo version and the general specification was similar to that of the 250 P. Some modifications were made

Above left: The 250 P was introduced in late 1962 and had considerable success. Seen here at the 1963 Targa Florio, it came with a variety of different engines, was often considered to be really a 275 LM and was the forerunner of the 250 LM Berlinetta.

Right: 250 LM at Le Mans in 1965, placed first with Masten Gregory and Jochen Rindt sharing the drive.

to the bodywork as the model moved on to the London, Turin and Brussels shows. The roof line was less angular and had been lengthened and an air intake was let into the forepart of the rear wing to duct cool air to the brakes and carburetors; later this scoop was slightly enlarged but served only the brakes as the carburetors were fed cool air from the rear deck. It was a delightful looking car with a short nose, beautifully contoured rear wings and a slightly upturned tail across the back of the rear deck.

Ferrari had hopes that the CSI would homologate the tipo for gran turismo racing but they wouldn't agree as there was a certain looseness in the regulations which other constructors thought should be tightened up. Throughout his long battle with CSI Ferrari continued to refer to the tipo as a 250 LM and never accepted that it was, in fact, a 275 LM, giving the 40 or so cars which were built odd chassis numbers, a further indication that they were gran turismo cars as far as he was concerned.

Most of the cars were sold to customers and concessionaires who raced them with some success in 1964 with 10 major and many minor wins.

The 275 P and 330 P

For 1964 two new competition models (both spyders) were introduced, the 275 P with specifications similar to the 250 LM and the 330 P with similar specifications to the 250 LM, like six Weber carburetors, a 5-speed gearbox in unit with the differential, single overhead camshaft per bank of cylinders, a single plug per cylinder and coil ignition and with a power rating of 370bhp at 7300rpm.

Coachwork was in essence similar in each prototype to that of the 250 P, but there were varying treatments to individual cars and in some cases the 275 Ps were just re-engined versions of the 250 P.

Neither car appeared until the Sebring 12-hour event on 21 March with the 3.3-liter versions in the hands of Parkes/ Maglioli and Vaccarella/Scarfiotti and the 4-liters with Surtees/Bandini, Graham Hill/Bonnier and Rodriguez/Fulp driving. The Parkes/Maglioli car won at an average speed of 92.4mph with second place going to the 3.3-liter of Vaccarella/Scarfiotti. Surtees and Bandini took third place but the Maranello Concessionaires entry of a 4-liter prototype retired in the ninth hour with transmission failure after being in second place. A hose pipe burst on the Rodriguez/ Fulp car in the third hour causing overheating and a necessary retirement.

Next on the calendar was the Nurburgring 1000km held on 31 May when the Scuderia sent the 3.3-liter 275 Ps feeling that these cars would be more suitable to the circuit. Scarfiotti and Vaccarella won at an average speed of 87mph while the Parkes/Guichet GTO was second overall and first in the gran turismo class.

A large contingent of Ferraris contested the Le Mans 24-hour event on 20–21 June including 275 Ps and 330 Ps. Once more a 275 P took the chequered flag with Vaccarella and Guichet driving at an average speed of 121.6mph. Graham Hill and Bonnier in a 330 P came second averaging 119.7mph and another 330 P driven by Bandini/Surtees was next home at 117.3mph. Ferraris also filled the 5th, 6th, 9th and 16th positions, making the classic endurance race little more than a procession of Ferraris.

Enzo Ferrari had every reason to feel elated with the accomplishments of his competition cars during the 1964 season. The GTOs had won the Manufacturers' Championship, the 275 P and 330 P prototypes were unbeatable and the 250 LMs had come good.

Right: Test day at Le Mans in 1965. The 330P2 was probably not the most successful of the P series cars.

Below: The 365 series ran through at least seven different variants, all of which share similar characteristics and make them the Ferrarris which most look like the popular conception of the breed.

The 275 P2, 330 P2, 365 P2 and 365 P2/3

Ford had entered the European endurance competition scene with the Ford GT40 and its derivatives, and Ferrari was well aware of the threat to his dominance in the prototypes and gran turismo events so he countered with the 275 P2, 330 P2, 365 P2 and 365 P2/3 for the 1965 season. The first two models were basically for works use while the last two, being less complicated, were for concessionaires and privateers to race.

The P2 prototypes were quite new with the semi-monocoque chassis and the independent rear suspension derived from the formula 1 car. The bodywork for these spyder prototypes was developed from wind-tunnel studies and was not designed by Pininfarina. They were lower, with a more pleasing and sleeker line than the previous prototypes. The nose was nearer to the ground and to prevent any tendency to lift at high speed diplane spoilers were incorporated on either side of the nose. While the first car was fitted with a wraparound screen the later cars were given higher windshields and behind the driver the now familiar 'basket-handle' roll bar. Since the cars were so low to the ground it was necessary to have a bulge on the rear deck to cover the stack of the six twin-choke Weber carburetors atop the 4-liter V12 powerplant, based on an old design developed for the 1957 sports cars.

The first P2 spyder was the 330 with a 4-liter engine while the 275 P2 would use the 3.3-liter engine. For customers the 4-liter 330 P2 engine was bored out to 4.4-liters and the cars were designated 365.

Ferrari refused to enter his new prototypes for the Sebring 12-hour event. He was at loggerheads with the organizers who had included Appendix C sports cars which were powered by the big American engines. A number of private Ferraris were entered, 250 LMs, 275 Ps, 330 Ps and a GTO and the only one in the money (3rd place) was the 250 LM in the hands of David Piper and Tony Maggs.

10–11 April was Le Mans trial time and by then the Scuderia had a fully developed 330 P2 on hand for Surtees who proceeded to crack the existing lap record with a blistering 139.9mph, timed down the Mulsanne straight at around 190mph.

There was a big turn out of 14 Ferraris at Monza for the 1000km race but this was to be expected as it was their home ground. Parkes and Guichet took the 275 P2 to victory at an average of 126mph while Surtees and Scarfiotti had to be content with second place as they were plagued with tire trouble, although they were the fastest car and set the quickest lap at 133.7mph. Ferrari used the race to introduce the new Dino 166 P, a 65 degree V6 with twin overhead camshafts per cylinder block and a capacity of 1.6-liters. Baghetti and Giampiero Biscaldi had the drive but went out on lap 1 with engine trouble.

The next endurance event was the Nurburgring 1000km when the Monza result was reversed with Surtees/Scarfiotti taking the chequered flag in the 330 P2 with the 275 P2 of Parkes/Guichet following them home. The Dino 166 P now driven by Bandini/Vaccarella took fourth place although it had held third position at one stage. As there was some suspicion that the Dino's capacity was greater than alleged (obviously due to its good performance) Eugenio Dragoni (Ferrari team manager) had the engine taken down to be measured thereby proving its displacement was 1596cc.

On 19–20 June it was once again time for the classic Le Mans 24-hour race but although Ferrari recorded their sixth win in a row it was the privateers who made this possible as all the works cars went out.

Across the Atlantic the Bridgehampton Double 500 was run on 19 September and Pedro Rodriguez managed a second in the NART 365 P2 and Bob Grossman had a fourth place in his 330 P. The race was won by a Chaparral and third spot went to a Cobra. On the same day David Piper was at Mont Tremblant, Quebec, taking part in a 200 miler. He was second in his 365 P2 while Surtees won driving his own Chevrolet engined Lola 70.

Unfortunately for the factory the 330 P2 did not perform up to expectations so further work was necessary before the start of the new season in 1966. Nevertheless the other prototypes had done more than enough in the events which counted for Ferrari to take the Prototype title.

The 330 P3

The 330 P3 was a natural development of the 330 P2 and had a number of refinements, mechanical, chassis and body-work, in the hope that its competition history would be an improvement over its predecessor's. The engine was the same

4-liter V12 unit but Lucas indirect fuel injection was installed and with the compression ratio raised from 9.5:1 to 11.4:1 the output was increased to 420bhp at 8000rpm. The clutch had been moved so that it was now between the engine and the 5 speed ZF gearbox which replaced the Ferrari gearbox. There was some revision to the chassis which still followed the formula 1 practice, being made from alloy sheeting, steel tubing and some fiberglass pieces bonded together. Bodywork was also revised and the overall dry weight had been reduced to a useful 1588 pounds. With FIA rules changed as regards height and width of the windshield, a fairly wide choice was permitted and this suited Ferrari as it was molded, on both spyder and berlinetta versions, to give a smooth line from the front hood which obviously helped in decreasing the overall frontal area to assist wind-flow. The nose was very low, but not quite as low as the circuit sweepers of the seventies and eighties, with the radiator inlet across the full width. Head lamps, driving lamps and indicator lamps were clustered in a single plastic cover which was faired-in to the ends of each front wing. The line on the berlinetta from the rear of the driving compartment was smooth with good visibility through the rear windshield. The tail had a small airfoil and a high Kamm-type cut-off. Both spyders and berlinetta were beautifully proportioned with a height of only 38.8 inches, a width of 70 inches and overall length of 164 inches and the works claimed a top speed in excess of 190mph.

The 330 P3 made its debut on 26 March for the Sebring 12-hour race, in the hands of Parkes and Bondurant. For some time the car, in spyder bodywork, held first or second place but went out in the final hour with a broken gear-selector lever. The Ford menace was growing as their GT Mk.2s again ran out in first, second and third places but the 330 P3 claimed its first victory at the Monza 1000km on 25 April. Run in pouring rain, with day turned into night, the

Left: The Targa Florio in 1965, and the Dino of Scarfiotti/Parkes.
Below: All-new for 1967, the four-liter 330 P4 came in behind Ford at Le Mans (where it is seen here at White House corner) but took the prototype title for the season, beating Porsche by two points and Ford by a comfortable 12 points.

race average speed by the winners was 103.1mph and they also went on to complete the fastest lap at 109.2mph.

Spa-Francorchamps hosted the next round of the championship, again a 1000km race, on 22 May. Parkes and Scarfiotti again shared a 330 P winning at the high average speed of 131.7mph and they also set a new course lap record of 139mph. For the first time a Ferrari works car had been fitted with Firestone tires. The 2-liter class was won by a Dino 206 S berlinetta with Guichet and Attwood driving.

Once more rain fell during an endurance race; on this occasion it was the Nurburgring 1000km held on 5 June. This event gave the 2-liter Dinos a chance to show their real mettle for the Scarfiotti/Bandini car took second place right up the tail of the winning Chaparral 2D coupe (Phil Hill/Jo Bonnier) averaging 89.1mph against the winners' average of 89.4mph. Rodriguez/Richie Ginther, also Dino 206S mounted were third. The 330 P3, although making fastest lap at 98.6mph in the hands of Surtees, went out on lap 36, the clutch burning out. Transaxle trouble saw the end of the Maranello Concessionaires Dino 206S on lap 28.

The Le Mans classic on 18–19 June was a Ferrari debacle. There were labor problems at the factory so preparation of the cars after the Nurburgring race was minimal and as if that wasn't enough Surtees was dumbfounded when he discovered that Scarfiotti was down to share the drive of his 330 P3; he had only expected to have Parkes as co-driver. Team manager Dragoni explained this was a precaution as he felt that Surtees had not recovered fully from injuries sustained during practice for 1965 Canadian Grand Prix. A furious Surtees stormed off to see Ferrari at Modena leaving the Scuderia without their ace driver. For team discipline Ferrari had to uphold Dragoni's decision which was a pity for it had been Dragoni's attitude to Phil Hill earlier in the sixties which had made Hill decide to quit. For the race Ferrari fielded three 330 P3s, two Dino 206S were entered by NART and Maranello Concessionaires had one Dino for Salmon/Hobbs.

Four Ferraris had lasted up to the 18th hour but two hours later only two were keeping the marque flag aloft, one finishing 8th overall and first in the GT class while the other finished in 10th spot.

Ford had, at last, achieved two goals — winning at Le Mans and, perhaps just as important to them, beating Ferrari on what had become their own preserve; at the same time clinching the Manufacturers' Championship with 38 points (two ahead of Ferrari) while Porsche took the Prototype title. Ferrari did not contest any other race with the 330 P3s for the remainder of the season, as no title points were at stake but the other prototypes were still in contention.

1966 had been a season of mixed fortunes for the marque and it must have hurt Ferrari when the Le Mans race was wrested from him although he could with some justification lay the blame on the industrial unrest which had gripped Italy at the crucial time. There was no point in looking back so Ferrari set out on the trail once more to regain his supremacy over the Ford Motor Company.

The 330 P4

To prepare adequately for the 1967 season Ferrari took his new offering to Daytona for extensive practice. Parkes, Scarfiotti, Chris Amon (a new recruit to the Scuderia) and Bandini were given the job of testing and after a total of 580 laps they called it a day. The Daytona lap record was broken time after time and a top speed of around 210mph had been reached. The car was the 330 P4 with spyder bodywork.

The V12 4-liter engine to power the car was a new design based on an all new formula 1 3-liter unit designed by Ing. Franco Rocchi which had taken the first two places in the 1966 Italian Grand Prix held at Monza. The engine in 3-liter form developed 380bhp at 10,000rpm.

The 4-liter 60 degree V12 had twin overhead camshafts per bank of cylinders with three valves per cylinder, two inlet and one exhaust. Oil was pushed through the engine and scavenged by two pumps and thence through a chassis frame member to an oil cooler across the front of the car and returned via another chassis frame tube. Water for cooling was also taken from and returned to the radiator via chassis frame tubes.

Suspension was independent all round with transverse wishbones, coil springs with damper units and anti-roll bars. Brakes were ventilated disk-mounted outboard and cooled by air taken by large bore trunking from scoops in the doors and from slots on either side of the nose.

Two Scuderia 330 P4s were sent to the States for the Daytona 24-hour event to be held on 4–5 February. The spyder, which had been tested so thoroughly on the circuit the previous December was entrusted to Chris Amon and Bandini while Parkes and Scarfiotti had a new berlinetta. Like Indianapolis a rolling start was used and as the pace maker pulled off Phil Hill in a Chaparral led off but after 3 hours, hit a retaining wall and was out, while the 7-liter Ford Mk. 2s (of which there were six) all had transmission failures. The factory Ferraris only had minor troubles and at the finish toured the last three laps allowing the NART car driven by Rodriguez/Guichet to join them to cross the finish line abreast.

Ford had lost round one.

Once again on their home ground at Monza on 25 April the first cars home after 1000kms were the 330 P4s of Amon/Bandini and Parkes/Scarfiotti, both sets of drivers using their Daytona cars. All told 17 Ferraris had started from a total entry of 41 which at least gave them good odds! Ford was still smarting from the debacle at Daytona and

was determined to retain the 'crown' they had worked so hard to win at the 1966 Le Mans. This year they entered four new Mk. 4s and three older Mk. 2s with engine specifications similar to the Mk. 4. Ferrari sent three 330 P4s (2 berlinettas and one spyder). He also loaned a 330 P4 to Equipe National Belge for Beurlys/Mairesse. Thirty pounds had been shaved from the weight by using magnesium cases for the 5-speed gearboxes. NART, Maranello Concessionaires and Scuderia Filipinetti had their 330 P3/4 but with the new Ferrari 5-speed transmission. Filipinetti also entered a 2-cam 275 GTB and Chinetti's NART also had the long-tailed 365 P2/3.

For three hours Ford and Chaparral fought out the lead with the Ferrari holding back. At midnight the Parkes/Scarfiotti 330 P4 had moved into third place behind two Fords, but by 3 am the A J Foyt Ford was miles ahead of them. By 2 pm Parkes/Scarfiotti and Beurlys/Mairesse started to motor in earnest, reducing Foyt's lead by 10 seconds every lap, but the chase was useless. All the Fords, Chaparral and Aston Martin Lola were timed down the Mulsanne straight at 200mph or over while the 330 P4s could only muster 193mph.

Still, the final round for the Manufacturers' Championship took place on 30 July at Brands Hatch for the BOAC 500, and this race would decide whether Porsche or Ferrari (with respectively 32 and 31 points) would take the title, since Ford had only 22 points. Ferrari sent three 330 P4 spyders, Maranello Concessionaires entered their 330 P3/4 and there were three 250 LMs, all privately owned. After four hours the Phil Hill/Mike Spence Chaparral was in the lead with the McLaren/Siffert Porsche second and Chris Amon in the 330 P4 third. Taking advantage of the Porsche pit stop to change brake pads Amon slipped into second place and stayed there to clinch the championship for Ferrari by 2 points.

This was not the end of the Prototypes, except for the prototypes title, as Chinetti's NART car was returned to the factory to be reworked and made lower as it was the intention to run in the CanAm series (first started in 1966). But with only 4 liters against the 7-liter Chevrolet V8 Group 7 cars, it was rather a long shot.

The 312 P

Ferrari decided that he would enter the Manufacturers' Championship for 1969 and introduced his contender, the 312 P, during December 1968. It was a beautiful looking sports racing spyder resembling a scaled-down version of the 612 CanAm car.

The 2990cc V12 engine had double overhead camshafts per bank of cylinders, 4 valves per cylinder, a single plug, coil ignition, Lucas fuel injection and with a compression ratio of 11.0:1 the power output was 430bhp at 9800rpm. The 5-speed gearbox was in unit with the differential. Suspension was independent all round with double wishbones and coil springs. Unlike the CanAm cars the championship prototypes had to be fitted with headlamps for obvious

Above: The flat 12 (Boxer) engine of the Farina at Turin in 1971.
Below: The 312PB was a development of the 312P V12 and was built for the manufacturers championship series which it won in 1972. It is pictured here in the BOAC 1000 at Brands Hatch in 1971.

reasons and they were set low and faired-into the front wings.

The 312 P missed out on the Daytona 24-hour but a single entry contested the Sebring 12-hour driven by Amon and Mario Andretti. It made pole position and was leading after 3 hours but then had cooling problems and dropped to second place where it finished the race.

Next seen at the April Le Mans trials it did not live up to its initial debut at Sebring and could only muster a fifth fastest. After this disappointing trial it was expected to appear at Le Mans for the race in June with a berlinetta body.

At Brands Hatch for the 500-miler a lone 312 P lined up in the center of the front row of the grid. At the wheel, Amon led for the first four laps before being passed by Siffert's Porsche. Thereafter he ran in third place until a puncture relegated him to fourth.

Before Le Mans the factory was testing a smooth-outline berlinetta 312 P. It had a long sloping roof with slats over the rear deck and proved very fast in tests. Two of these appeared at Le Mans for Amon/Schetty and Piper/Rodriguez but bad luck and a gearbox malfunction put them out.

The 312 Ps were never raced again by the factory as Ferrari pulled out of the Watkins Glen and Austrian events. They were cars which always seemed to flatter only to deceive but perhaps if the works had run a full team of three cars the results might have been better. On the other hand the larger displacement Porsche 917s were reliable, apart from being fast, although the differential in speeds was not great. In any case Ferrari had already set to work to build the 512 S cars to counter the German opposition.

The 312 PB

These cars were designed to conform with the regulations of 3 liters for prototypes effective 1 January 1972. Being flat 12s their engine configuration can be traced back to 1964 when the factory introduced a 1.5-liter flat 12 formula 1 car. And while not exactly side-lining these boxer units it was not until the winter of 1969/1970 that the first flat 12 3-liter

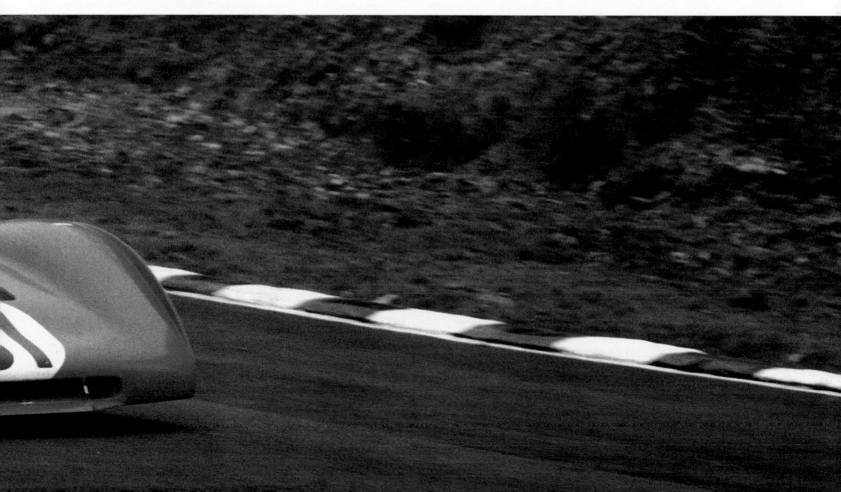

formula 1 car, the 312 B, was ested. The 312 PB sports racing car followed, and during tests in October 1970 it was given an aluminum body, this being easy to work on should any revision be necessary. When the time came to take to the circuits a fibreglass body was used. In early races there were no headlamps but these were added in time for the 1971 Sebring 12-hour race.

The 312 PB was really no more than a thinly disguised flat 12 formula 1 racing car but with equipment added necessary for sports car racing! Tuned for endurance racing and with a compression ratio of 11.5:1 the power output was 450bhp at 11,000rpm which was some 30bhp less than the formula 1 car. The chassis was the usual tubular steel structure covered with sheet aluminium. Body-work was in two sections and the front portion included the doors. The nose opening was to help keep the front end down and the two ducts on either side of this opening led cool air to the brakes. The water radiators were placed in the center of the chassis on either side of the cockpit and cooled by air intakes recessed in the doors. The oil radiator was atop the engine with two scoops on the rear deck and a larger slot feeding air to the engine compartment. On the 1972 models a low-placed airfoil stretched the width of the tail supported by two struts in a central position and held at the ends by two fins on the edges of the rear wings. The wheels were slotted alloy disk type.

A single car was sent to Buenos Aires for the opening round of the Manufacturers' Championship in January 1971 with Giunti/Merzario as drivers. During practice it qualified for the front row of the grid and led off the line for five laps until Giunti crashed into a stationary Matra; the Ferrari burst into flames. Giunti died from severe burns and head injuries and the car was wrecked beyond repair.

Jackie Ickx (a new driver for the Scuderia) and Andretti placed their 312 PB on the front row alongside the 5-liter 512 M of Donohue/Hobbs for the Sebring 12-hour. The 312 PB led for most of the first six hours when transmission failure put it out of contention.

Next race was the Brands Hatch 1000km and Ickx/Regazzoni had it on pole. Unfortunately, while in the lead, it took to the grass taking avoiding action from a spinning car. Ten invaluable minutes had been lost and despite some quick laps the car was still some three laps in arrears of the winning Alfa Romeo.

Somehow the 312 PB was having little luck, for at the Monza endurance race a third accident put the car out of the race. Ickx had made the front row again and led from the line but on lap 13 he hit wreckage from a Porsche 907.

The accident rate continued on the fast Spa Francorchamps circuit. Although the 312 PB could not match the speed of the 5-liter Gulf Porsches it was running a comfortable third when a slower driver in front of Regazzoni (who was travelling at around 180mph) decided to cut across his line. Result – another retirement.

The Targa Florio was given a miss but the repaired car from Spa appeared at the Nurburgring for the 1000km race. Ickx put the 312 PB on pole and was well into the lead before the half-way mark. But the engine was overheating and it was found that the cylinder heads had cracked. Ferrari decided to miss Le Mans (the 512 S and Ms represented the factory) and go for the Austrian race at the Osterreichring. The Porsches were off song so Ickx and Regazzoni were a good lap ahead of the chasing field after three quarters distance, but once again a race was lost as Regazzoni clouted a guard rail at a turn.

For the final championship round at Watkins Glen,

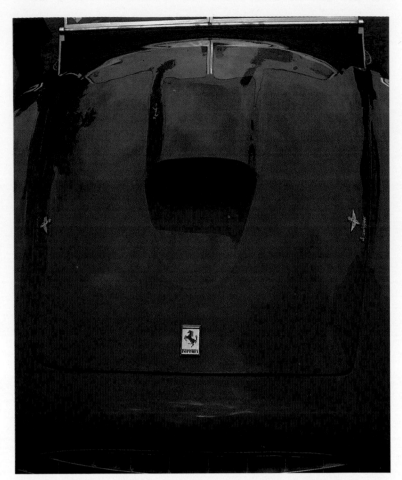

Andretti shared the 312 PB with Ickx. This time the car was relegated to the second row but the beautifully turned out Penske 512M (Donohue/Hobbs) had pole. After a few laps the 312 PB was running second (the Porsches again having an off day) but on lap 54 found itself in the lead for two laps. But, after a scheduled pit stop, the starter motor decided to call it a day with an inevitable retirement.

The results, championship-wise, were not satisfactory but the 312 PB had been proving itself all season and unless something drastic went wrong it looked all set to regain the manufacturers' crown in 1972 when the prototypes' capacity would be 3 liters.

There was to be an all out assault for the Manufacturers' title in 1972. Peter Schetty was appointed team manager and a further six cars were to be built so that while four (3 for each race and a spare) 312 PBs would be dispatched for each event another four would be at the factory preparing for the next event. Apart from their other factory commitments Ickx and Regazzoni would be a part of the team personnel.

The new car had 445bhp available, was light and very maneuverable. The competition was to come from Alfa Romeo, Mirage and Matra but the latter only contested Le Mans, reserving their assault for 1973.

The season started with the Buenos Aires 1000km race with a one-two for the 312 PB. Daytona had been reduced to a six-hour event and here again the 312 PB ran out first.

Further bodywork changes were made for the Monza endurance race; longer tails were fitted with full-width rear deck wings. Rain fell most of the time, flooding the track, and reduced the winners' speed by as much as 40mph from the previous year (around 146mph). Ickx and Regazzoni beat a Porsche 908/3 with Peterson/Schenken in third place. During the race most of the cars left the track at one time or another and unfortunately Redman/Merzario damaged their car too badly to continue after such an excursion.

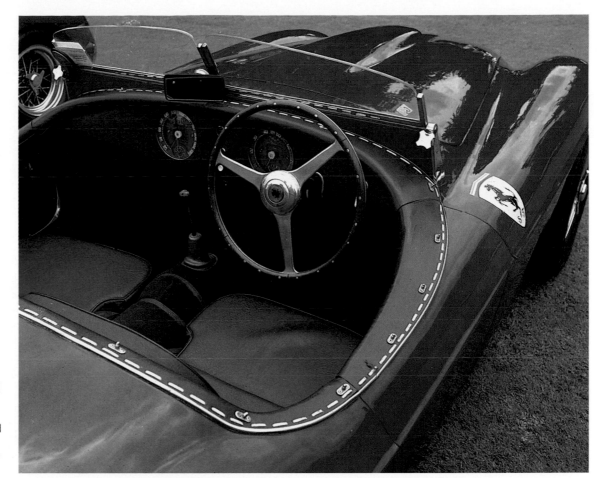

All pictures: The 212 was a 12-cylinder sports car which was campaigned during the 1969 European Hill Climb Championship by Peter Schetty when it wiped the board clean, and shared its development with the experimental 212 F1 car built for Rudolf Fischer. Information gained from this led directly to the larger-capacity 275 F1 and eventually the 312 F1 series.

Spa was the usual high-speed event without much drama apart from Peterson who found a damp patch on the circuit and crashed. As a change the Redman/Merzario car crossed the line in first place followed by Ickx/Regazzoni. Ferrari was no doubt in two minds about commiting a 312 PB for the rugged and arduous Targa Florio but at the last moment sent expert rally driver Munari to partner extrovert Merzario. They won with a margin of 16 seconds from an Alfa Romeo after a hard 492 miles.

The usual three car team went to the Nurburgring and for once they were matched for speed by a Mirage. The result, as on other occasions, was a one/two for the 312 PBs with Peterson/Schenken followed over the line by Redman/Merzario. Regazzoni crashed while being chased by a Mirage.

Driver changes took place at the Osterreichring and there was no 312 PB on the front row. All the cars, including the Ferraris, seemed to suffer from one problem or another but, for all that, the 312 PBs made it a 1-2-3-4 finish.

Watkins Glen wound up the season with a 6-hour race. Record or not Ferrari made it again with a 1-2 thus completing 10 wins in the 10 starts for the championship.

The 625 LM

The 4th Supercortemaggiore 1000km race took place at the Monza circuit on 24 June 1956 and was for sports cars with an upper limit of 2-liters. Three of these cars, the Testa Rossas, were entered for the event and all had Carrozzeria Touring bodywork. The cars were a Ferrari team effort consisting of Vittorio Jano, Alberto Massimino, Andrea Fraschetti and Luigi Bellantani who had taken over after the departure of Lampredi during the summer of the previous year. The Peter Collins/Mike Hawthorn team won with Fangio/Castellotti third and Genebien/de Portago 4th. At Le Mans, one month later, the same cars were on hand but had been fitted with 2.5-liter engines which were identical to the 625 formula 1 units. The organizers had insisted that entrants proved 100 cars had been built of the type entered but, of course, Ferrari could not show any such proof and they were entered as prototypes and designated 625 Le Mans. In view of their lack of power — only 225bhp at 6200rpm and their maximum speed down the Mulsanne straight of approximately 144mph against the 156mph of the D type Jaguars, they came in a creditable third and fourth.

The 330 LMB/330 LM

The World's Sports Car Championship was dropped for 1962 when a new championship for gran turismo cars was instituted. Those responsible for the new rules were in some doubt as to whether the championship would attract sufficient entries and — just as important — enough interest for the motoring press and spectators. In view of this the rules were sufficiently flexible to include the up to 3-liter sports cars and experimental or prototype gran turismo cars of up to 4-liters.

At the Nurburgring and Le Mans 1962 the factory ran a 4-liter car which from the outward appearance could hardly be distinguished from a GTO. In a press release before the Le Mans race Ferrari gave it the designation 330 LM berlinetta and the 4-liter engine was of the type used for the 400 Superamerica gran turismo cars.

At his press conference early the following year (1963) a development of the 330 LMB was shown. The new offering had an engine similar to that of the 1962 car but the chassis was new and the wheelbase had been increased. The car was designated 330 LM and was clothed with beautiful bodywork which was a combination of the best features of the GTO and the 250 GT berlinetta Lusso. The front was pure GTO with the aggression displayed by that car and the rear had the softer flowing line of the Lusso.

The front mounted V12 unit had a displacement of 3967cc, a single overhead camshaft per bank of cylinders, a single plug for each cylinder, coil ignition and 6 Weber 42 DCN carburetors (for the 1962 Le Mans car and the three 1963 cars) while the 1962 Nurburgring car had 3 Weber 46 DCF3 carburetors. The 4-speed gearbox was in unit with the differential. Front suspension was independent with double wishbones and coil spring with a rigid rear axle with semi-elliptic springs.

The 212 E Montagna/Sport 2000

This one-off flat 12 was a development from the 1.5-liter formula 1 car of 1965 but was enlarged to 2-liters in 1967 using one of the Dino 206 S spyder chassis. Originally designated the Sport 2000, its purpose was to compete in the 1968 European Mountain Championship but for one reason or another it did not run. It reappeared in 1969 using a developed Dino 206S chassis and was then designated 212 E Montagna.

The flat 12 boxer engine had been developed by Jacoponi and had a displacement of 1990.8cc, double overhead camshafts per bank of cylinders, single plug, coil ignition, 4 valves per cylinder, Lucas fuel injection and a compression ratio of 11.0:1. It delivered 320bhp at 11,800rpm. The 5-speed gearbox was located behind the mid-mounted engine. Front suspension was independent with double wishbones and coil springs while at the rear there was a single upper arm with a lower wishbone and coil springs.

For the European Mountain Championship, Peter Schetty took the wheel and, winning 7 out of the 8 rounds, was unbeatable, collecting new records on the way. The car, having already easily won the championship, did not turn up for the final event.

The Dino 166 P and 206 S

Except in the early years when Ferrari reigned supreme, he had shown little interest in formula 2. During 1964 the CSI decided on a change of displacement for formula 2 racing to take effect from 1 January 1967. It is probable that Ferrari took a hard look at what the new formula for cars with a capacity of up to 1600cc might do for his commercial prospects world-wide, having noted Porsche's sales with smaller displacement gran turismo cars.

With this in mind Ferrari made a deal with FIAT for them to produce a small engine which, as it turned out, benefited both parties financially.

At his press conference in December 1964 Ferrari made an oblique reference to the production of a 168 Dino GT with a view to the possibility of building a 1600cc V8 and said he would give further details during 1965. It was thought that this car would be based on the 1500cc V8 with which John Surtees had won the 1964 World Drivers Championship. Some five months later the factory came up with the Dino 166 P coupe which made its debut at Monza for the 1000km race on 25 April. The 65 degree V6 double overhead camshaft engine placed behind the cockpit was in-line and had a swept volume of 1592cc. Carburation was by 3 Weber twin-choke downdraft 38 DCNs with coil ignition by two Marelli distributors. With two plugs per cylinder and a compression ratio of 9.8:1 the power output was around 180bhp at 9000rpm. The 5-speed gearbox was in unit with the differential. Suspension was independent all round with double wishbones and coil springs. The chassis was a lightweight multi-tubular framework with riveted-on stress panelling. Dunlop disk brakes were carried outboard at the front and inboard at the rear.

Ferrari unveiled two cars at his press conference in February 1966 – the 330 P3 and the Piero Drogo Carrozzeria Sports Car bodied Dino 206 S.

The 206 S engine had been much modified although it still retained the 65 degree V6 and used the same bore and stroke of the mountain unit. The combustion chamber form had been improved and the compression ratio reduced from

Beautifully restored, this handsome 206 Dino, seen in the pit road at Brands Hatch, is the property of Pink Floyd superstar and serious race competitor Nick Mason, who has turned in creditable performances at the classic Le Mans 24 hours.

12.8:1 to 10.8:1. A single plug replaced the two plug ignition and the prototype had 3 Weber 40 DCN2 carburetors subsequently replaced by the 42 DCN 2. Fuel injection trials were being carried out. The power output was quoted as 218bhp at 9000rpm. The 5-speed gearbox was in unit with the differential. Suspension was independent all round with double wishbone and coil springs. While the car was slightly longer it had the same wheelbase and rear track of the 166/206 P, although the front track had been increased by 12mm to 1360mm.

The coachwork can only be described as a scaled-down version of the 330 P3, being beautifully proportioned with elegant lines. Whilst the overall height was a little greater than that of the 166 P coupe the cockpit area was smoother from the bonnet line.

Their first appearance was at Monza for the 1000km race which took place in dreadful weather, making the screen wipers quite useless. The first outing was not exactly a success; one works car managed a ninth place and the Maranello Concessionaires entry was placed 13th.

There was every intention of building 50 of this tipo for homologation as a 2-liter Group 4 Sports car but there was a great deal of industrial unrest in Italy at the time which not only affected production of all cars but also the preparation of the racing and sports racing car. Also Ferrari, as was his habit, was trying to combine formula 1 racing with sports car racing and these factors had ·a detrimental effect all round.

Some 18 206S prototypes were built with varying modifications either made singly or in various combinations; there were one or two plug engines, a choice between carburetors or fuel injection and as a final touch some units had 3 valve heads.

Competition GTBs

The 340 Mexico was a sportscar aimed particularly at the American market, one of a series – 340 America and 340MM were the others – which were campaigned on a limited basis in European endurance events like the Mille Miglia, but which met with considerable success in the hands of private entrants in the United States.

V12s front-engined up to 3 liters

Ferrari started racing sports cars shortly after he formed his own Scuderia in December 1929 but these were not, of course, his cars but either Alfa Romeos owned by wealthy young Italians who raced under the Scuderia banner or cars which he raced for the Alfa Romeo company.

When he severed his connection with Alfa Romeo in 1938 he formed his own company, Auto-Avio Construzioni, and he still had a number of friends around him, all well versed in automobilism, and more than willing to assist in the building, from FIAT parts, of two sports racing cars for the 1940 Mille Miglia. They were the eight-in-line Vetture 815.

Come the end of the 1939–45 war Ferrari was all ready to restart in the racing game and in November/December 1946 number of the Italian journal *Inter-Auto* there were details of a Ferrari engine intended for use in competition sports cars and with some tuning for single-seat racing cars. The specification was for a V12 with the included angle between the cylinder blocks set at 60 degrees.

The 166 Spyder Corsa/166 Mille Miglia

The 166 series was introduced in 1948 with a capacity of 1995cc. The Spyder Corsa had cycle type wings and was used for sports racing but could be used for formula 2 with the wings removed. Probably 10 of these cars were built before being replaced by a series of spyders with Superleggera bodies by Touring.

There were two groups of these 166 Mille Miglia with somewhere around 30 in the first, built between 1940 until late 1951 mainly with Touring bodies and the second of possibly 12 cars constructed from late 1952 into 1953 were, in the main, spyders with Vignale bodies. However, among the 42 or so all told, there were a dozen closed coupes.

Although all these early V12 Ferraris had a small swept volume they were more than a match for a number of the larger capacity racing cars. In 1948 their main victories were in the Targa Florio (Clemente Biondetti), Mille Miglia (Biondetti), Paris 12-hour (Chinetti).

Above and left: The 166 Corsa Spyder with its V6 configuration and three Weber carburettors typical of the elegant period.

Right: The 250 Testa Rossa was one of the works' most successful sports racing cars and was campaigned throughout the years 1958-62.

During 1949 there wasn't a sports car to match the 166 MM, which continued its winning ways from 1948. The Targa Florio was again the preserve of Biondetti and in the Mille Miglia Biondetti and Bonetto posted a one-two while Chinetti and Lord Selsdon won the Le Mans in a 166 barchetta. Chinetti then went on to win the Spa Francorchamps 24-hour event in July.

The 212 Export

There were two models of the 212 introduced in late 1950 — one, the Inter, was for sale as a road version while the Export was for racing. Both models were in production into 1953 with about 110 built altogether with bodies by Touring, Ghia, Vignale and Pinin Farina, with Vignale having the greatest share.

1951 began well for the 212 Export with Vittorio Marzotto and Piero Taruffi taking first and second places in the Tour of Scily in April, while, later in the month, Luigi Villoresi won the Coppa Inter-Europa. Although Piero Scotti could only make 3rd place in the Mille Miglia the race was still won by a Ferrari — the 340 America — driven by Villoresi. After this the tipo had a lean time but made a comeback in September when Franco Cornacchia was 2nd in the Targa Florio and Bobbie Baird won the Tourist Trophy in England. Perhaps its greatest success came in November when two 212 Exports were placed first and second in the rough and tough long distance Carrera Panamericana with Taruffi/Chinetti winning, the second car being handled by Alberto Ascari/Villoresi.

The 250 MM

Based on the 250 Sport this tipo was displayed in chassis form at the Paris Salon in September 1952 and was intended for competition by customers. There were 17 Pinin Farina coupes, 13 Vignale spyders and 1 Vignale coupe.

The V12 engine had a capacity of 2953cc and followed the almost universal specification of earlier cars except that it had a 4-speed all synchromesh gearbox and 3 Weber 36 IF4C carburetors. Power output was 240bhp at 7200rpm. Suspension front and rear was basically similar to the early sports

cars. It was not a fast car, having a top speed of 158mph but was extremely handy on any short twisting circuit.

Major competition successes for the tipo were hard to come by as a works car but in 1953 Villoresi gained a first and Farina a third at the Autodrome Grand Prix at Monza while Paolo Marzotto won the Dolomite Gold Cup at Belluna. In 1954 Trintignant and Piotti were first over the finish line in the Hyeres 12-hour race. Not surprisingly, as it was built for privateers, its successes in their hands were quite numerous wherever racing was to be found.

The 250 Mille Miglia was a most handsome car, in fact the best looker up to the time it was built and is now one of the most sought after by purists — which means that they command very high prices.

The 250 Testa Rossa

For the 1000km race at the Nurburgring on 26 May a new and important prototype sports racing car was entered. It was with this series, the Testa Rossas (a name derived from red crackle finish on the cam covers), that Ferrari pinned his hopes on regaining the Worlds Sports Car Championship for cars up to 3-liter displacement. He had also hoped that some of the production would be bought by privateers for competition, and felt that as the V12 gran turismo cars had been proving successful in races it was logical to develop the unit still further for sports racing.

It was joined for the Le Mans by a second prototype handled by Gendebien/Trintignant which at one stage was lying second until it was retired with a broken piston.

At his annual press conference on 22 November 1957 Enzo Ferrari introduced the 250 Testa Rossa for 1958. The V12 unit had a displacement of 2953cc, a single overhead camshaft per bank of cylinders, one plug per cylinder, coil ignition and 6 Weber 38 DCN carburetors. The 4-speed gearbox was in unit with the engine and with a compression ratio of 9.8:1 had a useful power output of 300bhp at 7200rpm. Suspension was independent at the front with double wishbones and coil springs and at the rear was a rigid axle with semi-elliptic springs.

The customer cars had similar specifications but were fitted with an elegant pontoon fender at the front which was introduced on the Le Mans prototype in 1957. This type of front end was not wholly satisfactory as it tended to lift on fast straights and after a production of 19 was abandoned in July 1958. These customer cars also had left-hand drive.

The works TR58 were entered for the Buenos Aires 1000km in January 1958 coming 1st and 2nd and driven respectively by Phil Hill/Collins and von Trips/Gendebien. The cars were similarly placed at Sebring but Musso replaced von Trips as co-driver for the second place car. Some modifications had been made by the time of the Targa Florio on 11 May. An all-enveloping body had replaced the earlier pontoon fender car, a 4-speed transaxle took care of the transmission and rear suspension was De Dion. This car was entrusted to Gendebien/Musso which led from start to finish with older types third and fourth. A really mixed bag of TRs arrived for the Nurburgring endurance race with old and new body shapes, old and new transmissions. Stirling Moss won in the lone Aston Martin but the TRs occupied 2nd, 3rd, 4th and 5th places.

Ten Testa Rossas were entered for Le Mans, nine being the V12-engined cars and one 4 in-line 500 TRC. Three of the V12s had the new transmission and De Dion rear axles and

one car also had a reversed hood air scoop. Hill and Gendebien won but the other two factory cars retired. Le Mans gave Ferrari his fifth World Sports Car Championship.

During the 1959 season significant changes were made. The wheelbase and bodies were shortened and high full-width windshields were fitted. Over the year both the Colombo and Lampredi-type engine had used hairpin type valve springs but now coil valve springs were used after Ferrari heard of higher reliable rpm to be obtained by the use of coil springs – standard practice in the States. It all seemed to work, as 300bhp was achieved with 8000rpm.

The season opened at Sebring on 21 March when the 1959 250 TRs took 1st and 2nd places, but at the Targa Florio race all the TRs seemed to suffer with rear axle failure and Moss won again in an Aston Martin at the Nurburgring.

Ferrari failed for the second time in the year at Le Mans when three team cars retired with engine troubles. Ferrari's cure was to adopt dry sump lubrication. At this point Ferrari led the Aston Martins by two points in the championship but at Goodwood for the Tourist Trophy Tony Brooks could only finish 3rd so the title went to Aston Martin.

There were further modifications for the 250 TR in 1960. All-round independent suspension for the cars appeared at

The 250 TR had a five-year career for the factory, during which time the championship fell to its V12 engine and superb handling in its first season, 1958, and again in 1960 and 61.

and an increased wheelbase. Two of the cars at Sebring had the twin nostril treatment while the third had the older nose-piece. Other cars entered privately were several TR/60s, including the 1960 Le Mans winner, driven by the Rodriguez brothers for NART, some front-engined Dino 246s, several 250 SWBs, a California Spyder and a new 246 SP having its first outing. Phil Hill and Genebien took the chequered flag with the TRI/61 with a hybrid TRI/61 driven by Mairesse/ Baghetti second, followed by the NART entry. Sharp and Hissom were 4th in a TRI/60.

Ferrari won the Targa Florio with the mid-engined 246 SP but Maserati won for the second year running at the Nurburgring. Ferrari still added 6 points to his score as the Rodriguez brothers placed their TRI/61 second. Third was a 246 SP followed by two 250 GT swb berlinettas.

Not yet totally convinced that mid-engined cars could be trusted he sent Hill and Gendebien and Parkes/Mairesse to Le Mans with TRI/61 cars which came first and second. NART's TRI/61 was present but third place went to the Guichet/Noblet 250 swb.

Although Ferrari had won the championship he sent a 246 SP to contest the Pescara 4-hour on 15 August. He also loaned a TRI/61 to Scuderia Centro Sud for Bandini and Scarlatti to drive. They won.

Its last major event was at Sebring 1962 when the TRI/62 (not an official designation) entered by Scuderia Republica de Venezia and driven by Bonnier/Bianchi took first place, ending the career of the 250 Testa Rossa and also the career of the front-engined competition cars apart from the gran turismo designs.

V12s front-engined over 3 liters

The 340 America

In the late summer of 1950 Ferrari announced his first big sports car, the 340 America and the brochure issued in October gave the details. Apart from the 275S, the 340 America was the first Ferrari, other than the formula 1 cars, to make use of the Lampredi 'long block' engine. The 4101cc unit was similar in specification to the 275 S but the power output was only 220bhp at 6000rpm.

The first tipo was on show at the 1950 Paris Salon. There were probably 25 examples built, including the two 275 S which were brought up to 340 specification. Touring built both barchetta and berlinetta bodies while Vignale built the coupes and spyders. During 1951 the 340 America scored two victories with Villoresi winning the important Mille Miglia race and Olivera the Portuguese Grand Prix at Porto on 17 June. A number of these sports racing cars crossed to the States where their owners won a number of races.

The 340 Mexico

In 1952 Ferrari built four of these cars, three coupes and one spyder built by Vignale for the 3rd Carrera Panamericana. The spyder was never entered for the race as it was bought by Bill Spear of the States and competed successfully in that country.

Specification was similar to that of the 275S and the 340 America but used DCF3 carburetors and had a longer wheelbase than the 340 America. They had a rating of 280bhp at 6600rpm.

This tipo had scant success and the race for which they were prepared was won by Bracco in a 250 MM. The 340 Mexico berlinettas (coupes) of Luigi Villoresi/Franco Cornacchia and Ascari Giuseppe Scotuzzi did not finish.

the annual Le Mans trials and the wheelbase was shortened even further. To comply with the FIA regulations high full width windshields plus wipers (much disliked by all drivers) were fitted. Because of the new dry sump lubrication system and a new 4-speed all indirect-geared transmission the engine was placed lower in the chassis. Since all-round independent suspension was used these cars were now designated TRI/60.

1961 saw a complete revision of bodywork for the 250 Testa Rossa when Carlo Chiti replaced Andrea Fraschetti, who was killed while testing way back in 1957 as design engineer. Chiti had a wind tunnel installed and is probably best known for his early body designs on the mid-engined specialized SP cars. He lowered the nose on the TR61 cars and added the distinctive touch of the twin nostril. The rear deck behind the cockpit was raised and a spoiler added across the width of the Kamm tail to deflect the noxious fumes of the burnt fuel from the exhaust pipes on deceleration.

There were five events counting towards the World Sports Car Championship in 1961. Sebring on 25 March came first with three of the new TR/61s entered. The chassis was a space frame with independent suspension all round

The 340 MM

The tipo was a more powerful version of the 340 Mexico with 300bhp available. There was a slight difference in specification using Weber DCF instead of DCF3 carburetors. The wheelbase was shortened but the front track was extended.

It was Villoresi who first brought success to the 340 series when he won the Tour of Sicily in April with a 340 MM and later in the month, on the 26th, Gianni Marzotto won the Mille Miglia with Tom Cole in fourth place and Giulia Cabianca ninth.

With these two failed tipos, although they could not be matched for sheer speed, Ferrari had some thinking to do before going back to the design board. While he might have improved the chassis what was really required was probably more development of existing components. How often, over the years, have we seen a tipo shelved before it has been fully developed?

The 375 MM and 375 Plus

Le Mans 1953 saw the initial appearance of the 375 MM driven by Ascari/Villoresi. The berlinetta was bodied by Pinin Farina on a long wheelbase and had the looks of a stretched 250 MM. It was said by the pit staff that the engine was a development of the car prepared for the 1952 Indianapolis 500. The car set the lap record but retired when plagued by clutch problems. Also at Le Mans were two 340 MM berlinettas and these were brought up to 375 specification. There was also a Vignale spyder 375 MM and the four cars represented the works for 1953.

The V12 had a displacement of 4494cc. Magneto ignition replaced coil and the 3 Webers were type IF/4C or 42 DCZ carburetors. A 4-speed gearbox was in unit with the engine. There were two versions – the works and customer cars and the works car had a power output of 320bhp at 7000rpm.

1954 saw a more powerful Ferrari, the 375 Plus. The compression ratio was increased slightly to 9.2:1 and three Weber 46 DCF3 twin choke carburetors were fitted. Power rating showed a minimum increase over the 375 MM from 320 to 344bhp but the mid-range power and flexibility of the engine had been improved. The displacement was now 4.9-liters and the 4-speed all synchromesh gearbox was in unit with the differential, the rear axle being a De Dion type located by parallel trailing arms.

The 1954 race record of the 375 Plus was adequate but it did win two events of importance – Le Mans in June with Gonzales and Trintignant driving and in November Umberto Maglioli won the grueling Carrera Panamericana.

The actual number of 340 MMs built is difficult to assess and the nearest count is between 12 and 18 with most bodies built by Pinin Farina either as berlinettas or spyders. Only four 375 Plus were built, all spyders, by Pinin Farina.

The 290 MM

A new Ferrari V12 powered the 290 MM and the engineering team now led by Vittorio Jano developed the best features from the Colombo and Lampredi engines and also used a number of components from the earlier cars. A displacement of 3490cc, twin ignition with 24 plugs and 4 distributors, 3 Weber 40 DCF carburetors and a compression ratio of 9.1:1 gave an output of 320bhp at 7300rpm. A 4-speed gearbox was in unit with the differential. Front suspension was double wishbones and coil springs while at the rear was a De Dion tube and transverse springs. Spyder bodies built by Scaglietti to a Pinin Farina design were similar to those of the 860 Monza.

For the important Mille Miglia the works entered five teams. The race was held in appalling weather on 29 April. Fangio and Castellotti each had the new 290 MM, Collins and Musso an 860 Monza apiece while Gendebien drove a Scaglietti lightweight 250 GT berlinetta. The performance by the team was really impressive as was the finishing order – Castellotti, Collins, Musso, Fangio and Gendebien in the first five places.

The 1000km Sports Car Grand Prix of Sweden run on the Kristianstad circuit hosted the final round of the championship and it was the decider for 1956. Ferrari fielded three 290 MMs. During the race Manson (not down to drive) but acting as a relief for Collins, had an oil line break spewing

The 340 MM was the spyder version of the 340 America introduced in 1950, but it never realized its full potential, as the factory turned their attention to the larger-capacity 375 MM the following year.

oil on the track and, spinning on the lubricant, shot off the circuit into a wheat-field. Collins (in another car) and Phil Hill were behind, hit the oil and also found themselves in the field but regained the circuit. There was much swapping of cars/drivers but Trintignant and Phil Hill brought the V12 home first and Ferrari, taking five of the first six places, made sure of the championship.

The 315 Sport and 335 Sport

Only two were built and both were entered for the 1957 12-hour Sebring race. The cars showed a good turn of speed but suffered various mechanical maladies and could only muster a 6th and 7th place.

Drivers for the Mille Miglia in May were Collins/Klemantaski, de Portago/Ed Nelson and Piero Taruffi (solo). Von Trips, also solo, had a 315 Sport and Gendebien/Wascher a very potent GT berlinetta with a new body style. Collins went out with rear axle failure before Brescia and the unfortunate de Portago had a front tire blow-out 25 miles from the finish killing himself, his co-driver and 10 spectators. Taruffi at the age of 51 and desperate to win at the thirteenth attempt won at an average of 94.8mph. Von

Trips could have passed Taruffi with his faster car but held back and followed him home with the incredibly fast GT berlinetta third at an average of 93.6mph.

Due to the de Portago tragedy two of the 335s were impounded for inspection so only one was present at the Nurburgring for the 1000km on 26 May. Tony Brooks in an Aston Martin DBR1/300 won.

For Le Mans Hawthorn/Musso shared a 335 Sport but retired with loss of oil pressure after setting a new lap record of 126mph. The 315 Sport managed fifth place driven by Stuart Lewis-Evans/Severi.

The 335 Sports were handled by Hawthorn/Musso and Phil Hill/Collins for the Swedish Grand Prix on 11 August but could only make 2nd and 3rd respectively behind the winning Maserati 400S.

Two 335 Sports and two 250 Testa Rossas contested the 3rd Venezuela Grand Prix. All the Ferraris were look-alike but the 4-liter cars had a small air scoop on the engine lid. The main opposition came from the Maseratis but they were left in disarray literally with crashed and burnt out cars strewn around the circuit! The Ferraris made it a 1, 2, 3, 4 and once more took the Championship.

V6 front-engined

The Dino 206S

It is said that the Dino sports cars came as a great surprise to all. On 7 April 1958, at the BARC Easter Monday meeting at Goodwood, Ferrari unloaded the 2-liter V6 front-engined Dino. Collins was there to drive the car for the Sussex Trophy race and to the surprise of all he placed the little Dino behind Stirling Moss's 3.7-liter Aston Martin DBR2 but ahead of Duncan Hamilton's 3.5-liter D-type Jaguar. The car was designated 206S. The 65 degree V6 unit had a displacement of 1983cc. Twin overhead camshafts provided the drive for two Marelli distributors with ignition by two plugs per cylinder. There were 3 Weber twin-throat 42 DCN carburetors and with a compression ratio of 9.8:1 the power output was given as between 220 and 225bhp at 8500rpm. These cars had no transaxle and the 4-speed gearbox was in unit with the engine.

The car appeared for the 40 lap 2-liter event at the Naples Grand Prix on 27 April but was retired with clutch problems after Musso had set the fastest lap.

The Dino 196 S

Ferrari had been discussing his twin overhead camshaft V6 engines with a well-known motoring journalist saying that the twin camshaft layout was too expensive. So it was not really surprising when the next sports Dino appeared with a single cam layout. In fact the V of the 6-cylinder engine now had an included angle of 60 degrees and the car was being tested late in 1958.

The engine resembled half of a V12 Testa Rossa unit but with some modification. The capacity was 1983cc and apart from a single camshaft per bank each cylinder had only one plug. With 3 Weber 42 DCN carburetors and a compression ratio of 9.8:1 it had an output of 195/200bhp at 7800rpm. The 4-speed gearbox was in unit with the engine. Only two cars were built, but it does appear that by building this Dino Ferrari had it in mind to have a small run of gran turismo cars based on the general specification. The bodywork was handsome, the design being by Pinin Farina and executed by Fantuzzi.

Race-wise the 196S was a failure. It appeared at Monza for the Coppa Sant' Ambroeus and in the 43rd Targa Florio it retired with gearbox troubles. Giulio Cabianca and

The 196 cars appeared in 1962, sharing the nostril nose with their F1 counterparts and their body style with the V8-engined 286SP. The 196 had a V6 engine of either 2 or 2.8 liter capacity and had a single camshaft per cylinder bank.

Giorgio Scarlatti were the drivers and they also shared the car for the Nurburgring 1000km on 7 June. On lap ten the engine blew up with either a holed piston or a dropped valve.

On 5 September the car contested the 24th RAC Tourist Trophy race at Goodwood but Scarlatti and Scarfiotti failed to finish. At the season's end during the Nassau festivities Ricardo Rodriguez placed the 196S second in an all-Ferrari race.

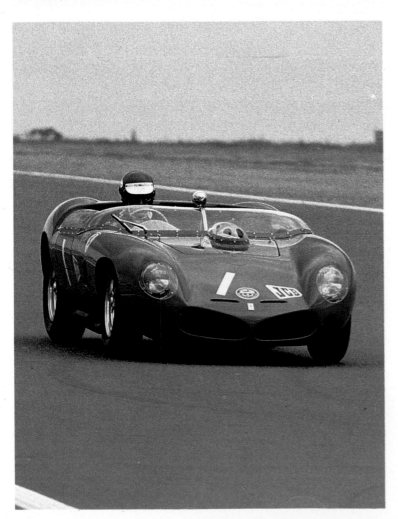

The Dino 246 S

For 1960 Ferrari had an enlarged engined Dino, the 246 S, with a displacement of 2417cc (bore/stroke 85 × 71mm) and still with single cams for the V6 unit. Full information on the engine is lacking but it was reputed to be rated at 248bhp at 7500rpm. As with all sports/sports racing cars for 1960 the 246 S had to comply with the governing body's ruling for full width high windshields so much disliked by the drivers. Like the 196S the new car failed to make its mark on the racing scene, not winning a single major event.

One car was sent to Buenos Aires for the 1000km race. It lasted 39 laps before the ignition caused problems. At Sebring the Rodriguez brothers had to drop out when the clutch gave trouble. It did look as if the 246 S would come good at the 44th Targa Florio for in the hands of Phil Hill/von Trips it ran a very good second to Bonnier's Porsche.

So ended the careers of the four Dino sports cars but it was hardly surprising that they were failures as the works could not have been expected to carry out much in the way of development on them. Their hands must have been full looking after the grand prix cars, preparing and developing the V12 Testa Rossas (after all Ferrari was much involved with the Sports Car Championship) and since the 250 GT berlinettas were showing such promise in the important gran turismo events the works had to service and repair these customer competition cars. The enterprise might have seemed costly at the time but surely Ferrari benefited in the long run when the mid-engined V6 SP cars took to the circuits.

In-line-fours

Ferrari's practice from the earliest days was to design and build engines which could be used, with modifications, for grand prix and sports/sports racing cars and also for gran turismo automobiles. All of which kept down the overall cost of development work and components and at the same time allowed engines to be switched for whatever purpose they were required. When, in 1951, Lampredi was given the task of designing the 2-liter 4-cylinder engine for formula 2

Left: The 196 entered competition in the 1962 Targa Florio in the 2-liter class with Bandini and Baghetti driving to a class win and second overall. First place in the race went to a 246SP (bottom left) driven by Mairesse and Gendebien.

Bottom right: The 500 Modial Spyder was introduced in 1955, using the power unit from the 1952/3 F2 cars, but it met with strong opposition from Maserati. Despite extra bhp gained from new heads and carburettors, it was still not as competitive as it should have been.

The original 4-cylinder unit had a displacement of 1985cc with twin overhead camshafts, two plugs per cylinder, magneto ignition and 2 Weber 40 DCOA/3 carburetors. With a 9.2:1 compression ratio the power was rated as 160bhp at 7000rpm. A few changes were made for the second series, the power was increased to 170bhp, 2 Weber 45 DCOA/3 carburetors were fitted and a 5-speed gear box installed. Probably 30 cars were built with the major portion having Scaglietti spyder bodies and a few spyders from Pinin Farina. It is believed that the first Scaglietti body for a Mondial was designed by Dino Ferrari.

The race record in 1953 was most encouraging with a 1st in Class and 2nd overall in the Casablanca 12-hour event on 20 December. At Agadir on 27 February it won its class with Francois Picard at the wheel and later at Dakar it was again successful in its class and came 2nd overall. Entered for the Mille Miglia on 1 May the 500 Mondial turned in its best performance being placed 2nd overall by Vittorio Marzotto.

The 750/860 Monza

During the winter 1953/54 work started on a new four cylinder engine derived from the Type 555 Grand Prix unit — this was the 750 Monza. As with most Lampredi designs the cylinder head and block assembly, crankcase and sump were aluminum alloy castings with cast-iron cylinder liners screwed into the head to eliminate compression leaks. Displacement was 2992cc and 2 Weber 58 DCOA/3 carburetors supplied the fuel. With a compression ratio of 8.6:1 the power was rated at 260bhp at 6000rpm. A 5-speed gearbox was in unit with the differential.

The spyder bodies were designed by Dino and built by Scaglietti and it is estimated that about 29 were built.

The competition history of the 750 Monza is not well recorded which is strange since so many were built but it seems certain that on its initial appearance at the Gran

events and the 2.5-liter unit for the future formula 1 (which would restart in 1954) it was natural that the units would find their way into sports cars.

The 500 Mondial

The 2-liter formula 2 engine which had been so successful in 1952–1953 was the basis for the 1954 500 Mondial sports car which was for both works and customer competition. The first Mondial engine was installed in a conventional Ferrari chassis, probably that of a 250 MM. There were two series, the second appearing in 1955.

Premio Supercortemaggiore run over the Monza circuit on 27 June 1954 Mike Hawthorn took the chequered flag.

In 1955 a larger version of the Monza contested the Tourist Trophy race on 17 September with Castellotti/Taruffi at the wheel but it was never in contention. The car was designated 860 Monza with a capacity of 3431cc. With a compression ratio of 8.6:1 the rating was 310bhp at 6200rpm. The main specifications followed those of the 750 Monza but it had a 4-speed gearbox in unit with the differential. Probably around 10–12 were built to this specification.

The 860 Monza didn't do too badly in 1956 starting with the Sebring race in March when Fangio and Castellotti beat Musso and Harry Schell to the line taking 1st and 2nd places. This was followed on 8 April as Peter Collins won the Tour of Sicily in a 1955 model and then took second place in the Mille Miglia with Musso third in another 860 Monza while Castellotti won the event in a 290 MM.

500 Testa Rossa and 500 TRC

Lampredi, who had been with Ferrari from 1947 except for a period of a few months, left in the summer of 1955 and went to work for FIAT in Torino. Jano, who had joined Ferrari when the Lancia Grand Prix cars and their equipment had been handed over to the Scuderia, was now part of the new engineering team which included Alberto Massimino, Luigi Bellantani and Andrea Freschetti. They came up with a new 2-liter sports racing car – the 500 Testa Rossa. On 28

April 1956 Ferrari showed his new offering at the New York show and on 24 June three of the cars were entered for the 1000km Supercortemaggiore race at Monza, which was for 2-liter cars. The cars were bodied by Carrozzeria Touring, the first time Ferrari had used Touring since the 340 MM.

The design was similar to the Monza and Mondial which Scaglietti had built but they had exaggerated wheel arch cut-outs. The three 500 TRs came first, second and fourth respectively. At Le Mans, one month later, the TRs were equipped with 2.5-liter engines (probably those used in the 625 Fl cars) and Ferrari had to enter them as prototypes and designated them 625 LM. Although the Jaguars and Aston Martins had the legs of the 625 LMs the Trintignant/Gendebien car finished third.

Ferrari announced a new 500 Testa Rossa late in 1956

Color pictures: The 750 Monza was a development of the Tipo 555 which appeared in 1954 and was pushed aside the following year by the uprated 860 Monza – the first Ferrari engine which was not oversquare.

Below left: The 500 TR was the first of the Testa Rossa cars and appeared in 1956. by 1958 it had given way to the illustrious 250TR championship winner.

which was built to comply with the FIA's 1957 Appendix C regulations. The car was called, quite logically, the 500 TRC. Scaglietti was commissioned to build the bodies which were lower by three inches than those of the 500 TR.

The specifications (apart from the 625 LM) for both tipos were similar; 4 in line engines with a displacement of 1984cc, double overhead camshafts, 2 plugs per cylinder, coil ignition and 2 Weber 40 DCO/3 carburetors. Compression ratio was 8.5:1 and power output 180bhp at 7000rpm. The 4-speed gearbox was in unit with the engine. Front suspension had double wishbones and coil spring with a rigid axle at the rear with coil springs.

The competition Gran Turismo Berlinettas

From his early days as a constructor Ferrari had not only raced sports cars but also berlinettas in the same classes since such cars were basically sports cars with a roof. This could, of course, be said of some of the gran turismo berlinettas which came along at a later date and which were built specifically for long distance endurance events. The term berlinetta, in Italian, can be translated as 'little sedan' or more usually, in Europe, as coupe.

In very general terms the road gran turismo berlinetta was a heavier car, with more interior comfort and refinement than its counterpart, used almost solely for racing. This latter model usually had a lighter aluminum body with perspex for the windows and windshields, the interior stripped so as to be quite stark without any semblance of comfort and containing only equipment essential for racing.

By 1955 sports car racing had reached the stage where the cars were no more than two-seater grand prix cars. It took the tragic accident at Le Mans in that year before the FIA changed the rules to establish new classes for gran turismo cars.

The 250 GT LWB Berlinetta

Ferrari, as is so often the case, was prepared for he had been in production with a 250 GT berlinetta since 1954 with a long wheelbase chassis. The familiar 60-degree V12 Colombo-designed engine powered these cars which had a displacement of 2953cc with a single overhead camshaft, single plug and 3 Weber 36 DCL 3 or 36 DCX 3 carburetors. Transmission was via a single dry-plate clutch and 4-speed all synchromesh gearbox in unit with the engine. Front suspension was independent with double wishbones and coil springs with a live rear axle and semi-elliptic springing. With a compression ratio which varied between 8.8 to 9.5:1 the output was from 230 to 280bhp at 7000rpm.

Ferrari had Pinin Farina design some lightweight bodies executed by Scaglietti which, with variations, became the customer competition car between 1956–1959. The original design was based on the 375 Mille Miglia competition berlinetta but had tail fins added to the rear of the rear wings and louvers behind the doors. The fins were subsequently removed. The grille was fussy in design and the headlamps were exposed but slightly recessed in the front wings. Over the years the lamps were recessed further into the front wings and covered with molded perspex being faired into the wings.

The 250 GT long wheelbase berlinetta was named (but not by the factory) the Tour de France subsequent to De Portago's win in that event in 1956. In general terms the Tour de France was a tough event which featured six races on major circuits, two hill-climbs and a drag race, apart from the long distance timed rally. Ferrari had first won the Tour as long ago as 1951, was second in 1952 and 1953 and then had a sequence of wins from 1956 to 1961 inclusive. In 1960 Ferraris took the first three places and filled the first four in 1961!

Apart from the Tour de France the long wheelbase berlinettas notched up a number of memorable wins in its class in a variety of races from the Tour of Sicily to the Mille Miglia and was almost capable of holding its own against more powerful machinery including other Ferrari tipos. The 250 GT long wheelbase berlinetta is one of a number of Ferraris which will always be sought after by the knowledgeable Ferrarist and will therefore command a high price

Unveiled in 1955, Ferrari grouped three different cars under the heading 250 GT, and included the legendary GTO, the long wheelbase 250 and this short wheelbase 250 GT Berlinetta which, although built originally for competition, was used as a road car by many Ferrari customers.

in the market place. While the 250 GT short wheelbase berlinetta which followed is even more sought after it didn't have such a distinguished racing history, winning less races than its predecessor.

Before the 250 GT swb berlinetta an 'interim' long wheelbase berlinetta model was produced which displayed rather softer body lines indicating that a change of coachwork style was about to take place. It was a handsome car but only 7 were built before the short wheelbase car came on the scene.

The 250 GT SWB Berlinetta

The Paris Salon of 1959 saw the introduction of the 250 GT short wheelbase berlinetta, a development of the long wheelbase model (the different wheelbases being 2400mm and 2600mm). There were two versions — the road cars and the competition cars, both having the same engine specifications as the earlier 250 GT berlinetta but with varying equipment.

The competition 250 GT swb had lighter bodywork and obviously stark interiors while the customer road cars were built with steel coachwork, a more luxurious interior and softer suspension.

The lines of the 250 GT swb followed fairly faithfully those of the 'interim' berlinetta but the quarter lights had been eliminated and the rear from the back of the cockpit roof had a more rakish angle as the overall length had been truncated. It was a handsome and purposeful-looking car. While the customer road cars had steel bodies the doors, bonnet and boot (trunk) lid were aluminum.

Due to changes in body style and wheelbase the FIA did not homologate the 250 GT swb berlinetta as gran turismo cars until shortly before the 1960 Le Mans event. Previous to this it had to be entered in sports car classes. As already noted the race was a Ferrari 'walk over' taking all placings up to 7th except for 3rd. The first 250 swb berlinetta home was 4th overall and 1st in the GT class. 5th, 6th and 7th places also went to the berlinettas.

While Stirling Moss had had a contract for one race (in the fifties) from Maranello he did not run as he blew his engine in practice which was not a popular thing to do as far as Ferrari was concerned! However, in 1960, privateer Rob Walker had bought a 250 swb berlinetta which he entered in the 25th Tourist Trophy on 20 August. Moss drove and he not only won the race but a week later with the same car won again at Brands Hatch. The short wheelbase car

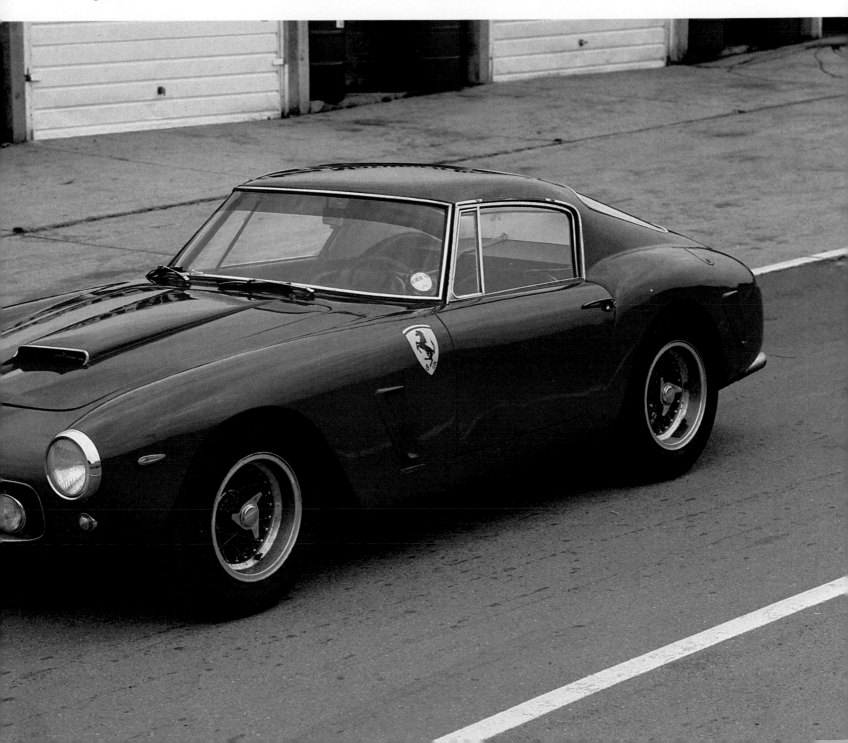

continued to win its races in 1960 and 1961 with an occasional lapse against such opposition as the Jaguar XK–E and Aston Martin GT.

All in all this was a tipo which combined ultra good looks with superb performances whether on the circuits, in rallies, hill-climbing and even as a static display in concours and will certainly live in the minds of all those fortunate enough to have seen it in competition.

The 250 GTO

In 1962 the FIA changed the rules for the Sports Car Championship and substituted two new categories; one for gran turismo cars and the other for prototypes. To qualify for the former at least 100 models were to have been built during a single year's production. Ferrari had been working on a new model for the new category, the 250 GTO, and being the man he was he persuaded the FIA that the new car was but a development of his 250 GT swb berlinetta. After all, where would the new GT class be without Ferrari participation? So the new tipo was homologated and the 'O' tacked on to the GT meant in Italian 'omologazione'. It was this new tipo designed and built by the factory engineering department which won the GT championship three years in succession (1962, 1963 and 1964).

The 250 GTO was a strikingly handsome looking car by Scaglietti with the long low nose close to the ground and the lamps faired into the front wings. Overall it was lower to the ground and sleeker than its predecessor, the 250 GT swb.

The car was shown to the press in February 1962 when it wore a nose to tail stripe of red, white and green (the Italian colors).

The 60 degree V12 engine with a displacement of 2953cc was based on the Testa Rossa unit and throughout its production used a dry-sump lubrication system. It also used 6 Weber 36 DCN carburetors. Drive was via a single dry-plate clutch with an all synchromesh 5-speed gearbox in unit with the engine. Suspension was similar to the short wheel-base tipo, although it has been suggested that coil springs should be used at the rear replacing the semi-elliptics but it was thought such a change might cause delay in obtaining homologation but coils were used around the tubular shock absorbers.

Sebring in March 1962 was its first outing when Phil Hill and Gendebien were 2nd overall and 1st in the GT class. For the race there was a small change to the bodywork as a spoiler had been 'tacked' on to the rear. All subsequent cars received the same treatment until the spoiler became an integral part of the rear end.

On 6 May the GTO was again 1st in class at the Targa Florio and 4th overall. At the Nurburgring on 27 May two cars were entered but one failed to restart after a pit stop (it had been leading the GT class) and the other crashed on the sixth lap. For the event the factory had also entered a prototype GTO of 4-liters (a 400 Superamerica engine with dry sump lubrication) which Parkes and Willy Mairesse drove to 2nd overall.

Arguably the most favored and sought-after Ferrari of them all, the 250GTO. The 250 GT series, introduced in 1955, was the subject of lengthy dispute between the factory and the race authorities, and was not homologated until 1962, with this car, designated 'O' for omologato.

Le Mans, two weeks after the Nurburgring, saw the Pierre Noblet/Jean Guichet GTO taking first in the GT Class and 2nd overall while two other GTOs finished 3rd and 6th overall.

The GTO continued to win race after race during 1962 culminating in the Paris 1000km run over the Monthlery track when they took 1st, 2nd, 4th and 5th places, the winning car driven by the Rodriguez brothers Ricardo and Pedro.

At his annual press conference in December 1962 — for the 1963 season — Ferrari had no new cars on show and intimated that only a few more GTOs would be built for, as he said, it was only the top drivers who could handle such fast cars. Production was limited to 39 GTOs including the three 4-liter cars over a three year period.

While the new car for 1963 was the 250 P which made an auspicious start at Sebring on 23 March, posting a one-two, the GTO continued to make its presence felt in all the important events including the eighth win by a Ferrari in the Tour de France! As in 1962 the last big event in the year's calendar was won by a GTO in the GT class in the Nassau Tourist Trophy and was also 2nd overall.

The 1964 version of the GTO was basically the same as the 1963 model but visually was very different but still extremely handsome and known as the Series II car. A wide air inlet at the front replaced the smaller elliptical opening with the additional air inlets on either side. The windshield was sharply raked and virtually a wraparound. The cockpit area was set well back from the long hood and the rear of the driver's compartment had sail panels which gave the rear deck the appearance of a sugar scoop. Three cars were built as originals and from the earlier production four chassis were re-bodied to 1964 styling.

The Series II GTO got off to a good start at the 1964 Daytona 2000km with Phil Hill/Pedro Rodriguez crossing the line first and followed home in 2nd and 3rd places by similar cars driven by Piper/Bianchi and Hansgen/Grossman respectively. This was followed up by a GT class win at Sebring on 21 March when Piper/Rodriguez/Gammino shared a 64 GTO.

The GTOs had plenty of competition in the GT class during the season with the Shelby Cobras, E-type Jaguars and Porsches to contend with, and at the Nurburgring 1000km the Ford Motor Company made its competition debut.

The season progressed with the GTOs still making their mark. The final event counting towards the Manufacturers' Championship was the Tour de France and once more Ferrari gained the honors with Bianchi/Berger first and Guichet/de Bourdon Y Parma in 2nd place, both in 1962/63 GTOs. Ferrari won the championship with the Shelby Cobras in second place.

Ferrari had still hoped to get the 250 LM homologated for 1965 but the FIA were adamant over their ruling so he decided not to contest the GT category that year. In fact it was suggested that the GTO would be the last front-engined Ferrari to contest the GT classes but it so happened that competition versions of the 275 GTB and 365 GTB/4 were built.

The 275 GTB/C

Two new models were on view at the Paris Salon in October 1964 – the 275 GTB (berlinetta) and 275 GTS (spyder) with coach design by Pinin Farina and built by Scaglietti. There was probably no intention to build a competition model as both were passenger cars and the first Ferraris to have independent suspension all round.

Eleven cars were built in 1966 for GT racing and featured

Left and below: The 250 GTO raced successfully between 1961 and '63 and includes a Le Mans win among its honours.
Bottom: The 275 GTB followed in 1966 and looks altogether sleeker than its more glamorous predecessor.

some of the changes made in that year for the production models such as a longer nose (which gave greater elegance to the overall shape). The body was aluminum alloy and with other weight saving some 150kg was knocked-off the normal passenger model. Bodywise it had a Lusso-type bonnet blister which covered the six Weber carburetors, the nose was certainly similar in some respects to either the GTO or 330 LMB.

The factory entered a car for the Nurburgring 1000km driven by Baghetti/Biscaldi which did not show up too well, although in practice Bandini had been much faster than the GTO.

The 365 GTB/4

Once more at the Paris Salon Ferrari was to spring another surprise although rumors of a new super car had been bandied about for some time. The date was October 1968 and the car the 365 GTB/4 with a Lampredi-based 60 degree V12 front-engine. It was probably the most exotic passenger car built by the factory and without doubt the fastest road car in the world with genuine top speed of 174mph. Pinin Farina had been the designer and Scaglietti, as usual, built the coachwork.

For a gran turismo car it was heavy, being about 1808kg (3615lb), but Luigi Chinetti, boss of NART, prepared a car for the 1971 Le Mans 24-hour race to be driven by Coco Chinetti and Bob Grossman. They posted 5th overall and it was thought they were 1st in the GT class but for some unaccountable reason a Porsche 911 was given as the winner.

This promising debut decided the factory into producing a few berlinettas which were designated 365 GTB/4A competizione. Weight had to be pared and this was reduced by nearly 200kg. Wide wheels and tires were necessary and the compression ratio was raised to 10.0:1 which resulted in a power increase from 352bhp/7500rpm to 402bhp at 8300rpm. Theoretically the top speed might be expected to be 200mph but whether this was ever achieved is doubtful.

The 4390cc four overhead camshaft engine had six Weber 40 DCN 20 carburetors mounted on the inside of the Vee. Two Marelli distributors sparked the single plug per cylinder and the 5-speed gearbox was in unit with the differential.

The Daytona, as the car was generally known, had one big fault — brakes which had a tendency to fade all too rapidly and this was certainly a disadvantage for any model intended for racing. The brakes were Dunlop ventilated all round, and the brake fluid would also boil. Chinetti added a

Right: The 365GTB/4 was the first works car to use the mid-mounted boxer 12 configuration.

Below: The 275 GTB was the first works GT car with independent rear suspension drawn from the 250LM, with which it shared some of its styling parentage; the other half was of course pure GTO.

Unveiled in 1968, the 365GTB/4 had caused considerable excitement even before it first appeared and had been nicknamed Daytona long before its launch at the Paris Salon. The name has stayed with the type ever since and the Daytona has remained a legend in GT excellence throughout the succeeding fifteen years.

dual master cylinder (minus servo assistance) and also better coil air ducting.

While the factory was never to enter a Daytona in a race they were more than happy to assist in the preparation of the cars used by their concessionaires, various equipes and privateers. In general the Daytona acquitted itself well as apart from its speed it was certainly a most reliable car.

The 308 GTB

Although the 250 LM could be called the first mid-engined car built by the factory for gran turismo class racing it was not until 1966 that homologation was bestowed on the tipo by the FIA. But it was really too late and in any case the 250 LM could not, in truth, be considered a GT car being in reality a two-seat racing car with a roof.

The 308 GTB is also mid-engined with a 3-litre V8 engine set transversely in the chassis. The 308 series which included the 308 GT4 2+2 and the Mondial 8 2+2. The fact remains that all the cars built in the series were passenger vehicles with no pretensions to being converted to gran turismo racing. A number have been raced by amateurs and semi-professionals but only at club level.

Apart from rebodying the chassis of the 308 GTB to the normal Group 5 configuration the main modifications were to the mechanics. To give a higher volumetric efficiency and some other advantages 4 instead of 2 valves per cylinder heads were fitted with the added boost of turbocharging. Using twin Garrett blowers, the Carma FF Biturbo 3-liter V8 had an outstanding power output of between 840 and

860bhp which was 'trimmed' for race purposes to 750bhp!

The race record is of some interest since it is the only 308 to have been raced seriously. At Daytona for the 24-hour event it set the fastest lap at 127.65mph before retiring with electrical and cooling problems on lap 4. Mugello saw the car in second place but an argument with a Lancia put it back a place where it continued until the engine gave up after 20 laps racing. Practice for the Monza event put the 308 on pole — the car had been timed down the straight at over 200mph. Unfortunately a turbo broke on the warm-up lap which put it out of the race. There was another retirement in the Silverstone race with a variety of problems. For the Nurburgring event the car was sidelined as it had been too badly damaged during practice to be repaired in time. Pole position was again achieved at Enna but it was 'flaming' on the third lap and retired once more. Kyalami was its last appearance in 1981 (it did not run in 1982) when after running for 2-hours of the 9-hour race the engine really blew up!

Perhaps with some help or advice from Maranello some reliability might have been built into the car. In any case Maranello must have watched its progress with some considerable interest and perhaps they are wise in not placing their faith in a turbo passenger car.

The 365 GT4/BB

The 365 GT4/BB was the first flat-12 mid-mounted engined berlinetta to be introduced by the works. Although displayed at the 1971 Turin show it didn't go into production until

1973. There can be no doubt that it was a fast passenger car built for comfort but not racing. Despite this there is always someone around willing to convert almost any berlinetta Ferrari into a race car and one of the first was always that old campaigner Luigi Chinetti and his NART outfit.

Since there is little evidence that anyone else wanted to race the model it may be assumed that the NART car was the only one ever to be raced and it is doubtful whether the factory was ever interested! The car was lightened by removing all unnecessary equipment and the body modified to accommodate the wide Goodyear tires. No doubt some work was carried out on the engine as the power output was alleged to be between 400–420bhp whereas the road versions output was 380bhp. Never competitive, it retired after covering one lap for the 1975 Daytona race but it did finish 6th at Sebring. At Road Atlanta mechanical failure put it out during practice and the engine caught fire at Lime Rock.

It was not raced in 1976 but appeared at Le Mans in 1977 where it finished 16th after a two-hour delay in the pits. Daytona 1978 was probably its last race when electrical problems set in so that it crossed the line in 22nd place.

The 512 BB

The 512 BB was introduced at the 1976 Paris Salon as a replacement for the 365 GT4/BB. Visually there appeared to be little difference but on close inspection the new car had a 'chin' spoiler under the front grille and NACA ducts low down on the body sides and just in front of the rear wings.

The flat-12 boxer engine was given an extra 552cc over the 365 GT4/BB model bringing the displacement up to 4942cc. But it was rated at only 360bhp – a power drop of 20bhp although the maximum speed was increased slightly to an estimated 188mph.

While the previous road berlinetta boxer received scant attention from the factory as regards racing, the new 5-liter

Above: The 308 GTS, a 3-liter V8 with classic sportscar lines, popular with customers and admirers since its introduction in 1977 as part of a range which was based on the 308GTB.

Right: Hailed by many as the ultimate in road-going cars, the 512BB was first shown at the Paris Salon in 1976. With 360bhp and a quoted top speed of 188mph it's by far the fastest Ferrari road car.

model was to have some encouragement. Ferrari had abandoned sports and gran turismo racing some years previously concentrating on formula 1 (a sign of Fiat influence perhaps?). Maybe Fiat were seeing the folly of this policy as Ferrari sales over the years had relied to a great extent on racing successes and not just from the formula 1 cars. Whatever the reason the factory gave support, even if it was limited, to a number of concessionaires and privateers wishing to race the 512 BB.

For 1979 the works stepped up development showing a greater interest in the car's competitiveness. Work on the body shells was carried out in Pinin Farina's wind-tunnel and the cars, now known as the Silhouette Boxers, were 16 inches longer (10 inches added to the nose and 6 inches to the tail). The headlamps were behind fairings within the front spoiler with the roof line continuing via a near horizontal sloping rear window right down to the tail which had an aerofoil across the rear deck supported by two vertical fins. The mechanics were virtually unchanged but with Lucas fuel injection the power output was 475bhp at 7200rpm. The gearbox, always a weak link, had stronger competition-type straight cut pinions. Water and oil cooling systems were enlarged and the transmission had its own oil radiator. The rear suspension was modified with two spring/damper units on each side with an American Indy type pneumatic jack mounted alongside. The cars were tested at both Fiorano and Fiat's Nardo tracks.

In preparation for the Le Mans race a great deal of testing took place, the Michelin tires being the main target. Four cars contested the race – two from Ch. Pozzi, one from NART and one from Ecurie Francorchamps. The Ferraris ran in the IMSA class (International Motor Sport Association), a cross between Group 4 and Group 5 as defined by the FISA. This meant that their main rivals were the turbocharged Porsche 935s.

There was some justification that the 512 BBs would do reasonably well at Le Mans after their initial outing at Daytona but the NART and Ch. Pozzi entries failed to finish. The two Pozzi cars crashed when trying to pass slower cars, one was lying sixth after 19 hours. The only finisher ran out 12th, having had a number of problems on the way.

Early 1980 saw two new 512 BBs on test at Monza; these had modified bodywork and mechanics. The body between the front and rear wheel arches below door level was extended downwards giving an impression of ground effects skirts. The main research on the engine was directed towards fuel consumption where a 10% reduction was achieved without reducing the power output.

Le Mans saw six cars entered (three 1979 models and three 1980 versions) – Ch. Pozzi took three cars (2 new and one older model) – NART a 1980 version which did not start as the engine threw a rod in practice – one Italian run under the Scuderia Supercar Bellancauto banner and the British ex-Ecurie Francorchamps car owned by Steve O'Rourke.

Wet weather during the early part of the race affected the electrics of the Ferraris necessitating numerous pit stops. Only two of the cars finished after various traumas – a Pozzi entry finishing 10th overall and 3rd in the IMSA category and the British entry lasting the 24 hours was 23rd overall and 8th in the IMSA class.

The 512 BBs did rather better in 1981 with two privately entered cars taking 1st and 3rd places in the IMSA class and finishing 5th and 9th overall. The NART and British entered cars were retired and Bellancauto had bad luck for the second year running, this time with 'disarranged' mechanics.

Above right: The 512BB was, like the rest of the Ferrari stable, quite fast enough to hold its own on a racetrack. This is Le Mans in 1981.

Right, above and below: A close look at the fabulous 512BB, showing how the whole rear body flips for engine access unparalleled in Ferrari road cars.

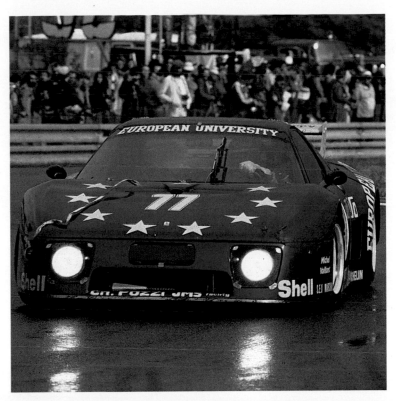

Although getting older five 512 BBs were due to contest Le Mans in 1982 but a private French entry failed to materialize. The familiar NART and Ch. Pozzi entries were present but perhaps the most striking car was the privately entered Ron and Patti Spangler Prancing Horse Farm 512 BB in Ferrari red with black and gold stripes and gold decals. Lasting the 24 hours it was placed 6th overall and 3rd in Group IGTX.

For a car which was built as a 'supercar' for road use and not designed for racing, all credit must go to the concessionaires and private owners who saw the possibilities of using it for endurance racing and to the works for giving some support even if it was limited.

Up to the present no turbocharged 512 BB has been seen on the circuits although one was entered for the 1977 Le Mans event. An unnamed Hong Kong enthusiast asked Louis Chateau to prepare such a car. Chateau had experience with the turbocharged Porsches but decided that as the 512 BBs lubrication system did not lend itself to conversion for racing purposes so the project was abandoned. Before the abandonment, however, a body had been built which was somewhat reminiscent of the Porsche 917. The car was given the 'code' name 512 Turbo GTP but had nothing to do with the factory.

Monaco in 1965, and Lorenzo Bandini at the wheel. He shared the Ferrari drive with luminaries like Hill, Surtees and Amon during his time with Ferrari from 1962 until his tragic death at the wheel in the 1967 Monaco GP. Inset: Hawthorn at the 1954 Spanish GP.

Formula 1

Enzo Ferrari has been in the racing game with cars bearing his name for 36 years and during that time his cars have notched up a total of 84 world championship races. Not a spectacular number perhaps but nonetheless a respectable total.

In 1958 a constructors' or manufacturers' championship was instituted and Ferrari has only won the title on six occasions – 1961, 1964, 1975, 1976, 1977 and 1979. He was also top constructor in 1952 and 1953 and taking into account the Lancia-Ferrari D50 in 1956 as well, although none of these years are to be found in the records. To round off his achievements he has been runner-up to the title in 1958, 1959, 1966, 1970, 1974 and 1978 and before the championship, in 1951. Statistics may be boring but the measure of the man's talents can best be set out simply by figures.

Apart from his constructors' titles seven of his drivers have won nine World Drivers' Championships (started in 1950). Alberto Ascari won the title in 1952 and 1953 driving the almost unbeatable 500 F2 and Juan Fangio in his only year as a contract Ferrari driver was successful in the 1956 Ferrari-Lancia D50. Mike Hawthorn just pipped Stirling Moss for the championship in 1958 driving the 246 and 256 Dinos and the only American to win the title was Phil Hill driving the 156 Fl. In 1964 John Surtees (seven times World Motorcycle champion) won the championship with the 158 Fl but it was another nine years before another Ferrari driver, Niki Lauda, was the title holder, winning in 1975 with the flat-12 312B and 312T and in 1977 with the 312 T2. South African Jody Scheckter who started off the 1979 season in the 312 T3 and had the use of the 312 T4 later in the year was the last man to become World Driver Champion in a Ferrari.

So much for the overall picture of how Ferrari has survived over the many years of his involvement in motor racing and it is to his credit that he has kept going even when nothing seemed to go right. He has on occasions made it known that he wanted no more to do with the sport but such pronouncements have been made by many sportsmen in the past in the heat of the moment. Ferrari's main protagonists have been the Italian national press (when winning ways are not forthcoming they scream abuse) and the governing body of the sport. Ferrari has always held a strong if not always a fair hand when dealing with the authorities, for any grid at a Grand Prix without at least one red car would not be a Grand Prix in the true sense.

The 125 Fl

While Ferrari had a competent group of technicians around him after World War II he was lacking a designer to enable him to fulfill his early ambition. Gioacchini Colombo was an obvious choice and a man whom Ferrari had known since 1924 when he joined the Alfa Romeo concern as a draughtsman. Colombo had progressed at the Portobello firm under Vittorio Jano but had become disenchanted with his position towards the end of the thirties when Jano had been forced out and replaced by an obnoxious Spaniard named Wilfredo Ricart. So the transition to help Ferrari when asked was not difficult.

Work on a 60 degree V12 engine started in 1946 and although a sports racing car, the 125 C, was the first to appear, in May 1947, the 1.5-liter supercharged racing car did not make its debut until September 1948 at the Italian Grand Prix on the road circuit at Valentine Park, Turin.

The first tipo 125 Fl grand prix cars were not exactly successful on the circuits but this could be said of many 'first-off' designed cars. Ferrari was lucky in having a great development engineer in his team – Luigi Bazzi – whose job it was to solve the problems as they arose.

The detachable cylinder-heads, block and crankcase were cast in aluminum. Wet cylinder liners were shrunk in and the heads held them in compression against the block. Each bank of cylinders had a single overhead camshaft and the exhaust and inlet valve per cylinder were actuated by rocker arms.

A single Weber 40 DO3C carburetor was situated in the V of the engine and the Roots-type supercharger was mounted at the front. With a compression ratio of 6.5:1 the power developed was only 225bhp which was well below that of its main rival the Alfa Romeo 158 with 310bhp at 7500rpm. The only way to compensate for the lack of power was to use a light tubular chassis. This was a ladder-

Left: The 125F1 was first raced in 1948, dominated the 1949 season and continued as a works car until as late as 1951, when it still had considerable success.

Right: The F1 120 race car.

type structure of oval section tubing with two main longitudinal members, a box section cross member at the front and, to support the aluminum body panels, tubular cross members and a welded framework. It had a short wheelbase which was a contributory factor to instability at high speed. Front suspension was by double wishbones of unequal length and a transverse leaf spring while the rear suspension incorporated torsion bars. Damping was by Houdaille vane-type shockabsorbers and the hydraulic brakes had finned alloy drums.

Three cars were entered for the 225-mile Italian Grand Prix which was run in appallingly wet weather with Farina, Sommer and B Bira as drivers.

Farina, when running fourth, lost control on the wet road and rammed some straw bales damaging the radiator, while Bira retired on lap 66 with transmission failure. Sommer took third place after a race-long duel with Villoresi's Maserati.

The Ferraris did no better at the Autodrome Grand Prix held over the Monza circuit but there was some consolation at the minor Circuit of Garda race when Farina won easily from Sterzi's Spyder Corse 2 liter car with Villoresi's Maserati third. The Spanish Grand Prix held over the street circuit at Pedralbes was another flop. Farina and Bira went out with transmission problems and José Pola blew his motor.

At the end of the season the works retained one car and built two new cars. The main changes were twin overhead camshafts per bank of cylinders, twin-stage supercharging, a longer wheelbase and a rear leaf spring over the rear axle. Power was increased to 300bhp at 7500rpm. The revised models were not available until late in the season for the Italian Grand Prix (also the European Grand Prix in 1949) at Monza on 11 September which Alberto Ascari won for Alfa at 105.04mph.

Without those main rivals, the Alfa Romeos, to contest the events for 1949 the 125 Fl had a fair season with five first places and two seconds with two top drivers — Alberto Ascari and Luigi Villoresi, who had good backup from amateur Peter Whitehead who had bought his car from the factory and received some support from Maranello.

The basic Colombo engine design was multi-purpose and this was evident during the early years when a number of sports cars were produced such as the tipo 166 Spyder Corse. The unit was also put to good use for formula libra and formula 2 racing cars. By increasing the displacement to 1995cc Ferrari had his tipo 166 formula libra car with a single Weber 40 DORC carburetor and single stage supercharger with an output of 310bhp at 7000rpm. The formula 2 car had the same capacity, no supercharger, three Weber 32 DCF carburetors and a power output of 155bhp (raised to 160bhp in 1950/51) at 7000rpm. These cars were highly successful in single-seat form, winning many races during 1949/50 and 1951, but the day of Ferrari's smaller capacity engines was nearly over with the departure of Colombo back to Alfa Romeo and his replacement by his number two, Aurelio Lampredi. Ferrari was not a man to continue along a set line when he could foresee advantages to be gained by following a new one although, at times, he needed convincing that new ideas would be to his benefit. At this time only a small amount of cash could have been coming his way with the sale of surplus racing and sports racing cars, for he had hardly touched on the commercial market for passenger cars, so an all-out effort would have to be made to gain world-wide recognition. This, he deduced, would be by advertising his wares on the racing circuits as other constructors had done in the twenties and thirties.

Ferrari had obviously seen the benefit to be gained by enlarging the capacity of Colombo's original design and discarding the extra boost obtained by supercharging. Supercharging meant thirsty engines which in turn meant more pit stops for fuel and to overcome the time wasted for refuelling meant a greater speed advantage over any rivals. He could also see that a large capacity unit would provide him with an engine that had a long development life.

Lampredi, who had been advocating the larger engine, was an empirical engineer. He had a 'feel' for automobile engineering which stood him well during the years he was with Ferrari and having had the benefit of Colombo's training was more than ready to tackle any new project. His job was three-fold — to design a 4.5-liter V12 unblown unit to beat the new Alfa Romeo 159, to prepare a 2.5-liter

Main picture and above left: The Tipo 500. This one, chassis no. 5, was raced by Alberto Ascari in the 1952 season.

four-in-line cylinder car for the 1954 season when new regulations for formula 1 racing would come into effect and finally to design a 2-liter four-in-line cylinder unit for formula 2 racing. The latter car was in part speculation but Ferrari had a suspicion that for 1952/53 the grand prix competition would be for formula 2 cars and not formula 1. As usual he guessed right!

The 375 Fl

Although Lampredi followed the basic design of Colombo's 60 degree V12 engine there were distinct differences. Known as the 'long block' unit, overall length was 42 inches (Colombo's was 37 inches).

The Italian Grand Prix at Monza on 3 September saw the race debut of the 4.5-liter 375 Fl. Cars were provided for Ascari and Serafini. Ascari's engine failed so he then shared Serafini's and they managed a creditable 2nd after a race distance of 312 miles. Two of the new cars contested the Penya Rhin Grand Prix over the Pedralbes street circuit on 29 October. Ascari won and was followed home by Serafini and in third place Taruffi brought his 4.1-liter 340 Fl.

Alfa Romeo had stayed at home during 1950 but came back to do battle with the 4.5-liter Ferraris in 1951. The 375 Fl had had a busy season racing in minor and major events and up to the time of the Spanish Grand Prix, run as usual at Pedralbes. On 28 October it was a 'toss-up' as to whether Maranello or Portobello would take the season's honors. There was not a manufacturers' title to be won as this was not instituted until 1958 but there was prestige to be won. Perhaps the odds were in favor of the Ferraris as they had scored a 1, 2, 3 the previous year over the same circuit, but for 1951 the race distance had been increased from 194 to 275 miles.

Ascari was on pole with Fangio (Alfa Romeo) alongside but tire problems beset the Ferraris. Fangio won and Froilan Gonzales snatched second place from Farina with Ascari 4th one lap down on the winner. So Ferrari lost the final battle with Alfa Romeo and Ascari had to be content with second place in the drivers' championship.

Having squeezed the last ounce of power from the Alfa's 159 engine and as the Italian Government had not been forthcoming with an expected subsidy to keep them afloat the Portobello firm had to say goodbye to top line motor racing for some 20 or so years.

With no competitors around, the 375 Fl cars were now obsolete as regards formula racing and buyers had to be found to get rid of them.

The 500 F2

As expected, the powers that be decided that the championship for 1952 and 1953 should be carried by the formula 2 cars. Ferrari was ready with his well-tested Tipo 500 F2 – a model that was almost unbeatable and bringing the factory a great deal of prestige.

Ferrari unveiled the 500 F2 in 1951. The four-in-line cylinder engine had a displacement of 1980cc with twin overhead camshafts, two valves, two plugs and two Marelli magnetos. The 1951 car had two Weber 50 DCO carburetors but these were replaced in 1952 with four Weber 45 DOEs and with a compression ratio of 12.8:1 the power output was 180bhp at 7500rpm.

In 1951 Ascari and Villoresi drove the new car in the Modena Grand Prix and dominated practice and the race although Villoresi had to retire at half-distance with engine trouble. Ascari won easily and set a new lap record at 75.53mph.

During 1952/53 the 500 F2 won 14 world championship races in a row and in 33 starts was beaten on only three occasions. Alberto Ascari became World Driver Champion in both years and Ferrari was top constructor.

The 625 F1

Ferrari had planned the new four-in-line 2.5-liter engine as far back as 1951 when the prototype unit for the 625 F1 was placed in the new 500 F2 chassis he was testing. The car was entered in the Bari Grand Prix for Taruffi to drive against heavier metal which included the 4.5-liter V12 375 F1s and the Alfa Romeo 159s. It finished in third place. Its next appearance was at the Valentino Grand Prix, Turin, in April 1952, when Taruffi finished second to Villoresi's 4.5-liter car. And in 1953, in three outings, it was first, second and third at Buenos Aires and with two cars entered for the Rouen Grand Prix was first and second. In a short sprint at Silverstone, over 50 miles, Hawthorn retired with an overheated engine.

While for many years now formula 1 cars have run on what is virtually pump fuel it is interesting to recall that the fuel mixture used by the 2.5-liter engine was 40 per cent methyl alcohol, 30 per cent benzole and 30 per cent 100-octane fuel with 1 per cent castor oil added.

Ferrari not only had the 625 F1 (the original 2.5-liter-engined car) for the new 1954 formula but was, in 1953, developing the 553 F1 car, also for the new formula. This tipo was called the 'Squalo' since its bulbous appearance was somewhat shark-like. An entirely new car, it was first tested at the Italian Grand Prix at Monza in 1953. The tipo was a further development of the original Lampredi four cylinder unit similar in many respects to the 625 F1. Weber designed a special twin-choke carburetor for the tipo, giving it two type 58 DCOAFs. Power output with a 12.0:1 compression ratio was initially 250bhp at 7500rpm from 2497cc. The 4-speed gearbox driven via the multi-plate clutch was in unit with the rear axle. Final drive incorporated a ZF limited slip differential and fuel was carried in side-mounted pannier tanks, which were part of the bodywork, and a small tank in the tail.

The 553 F1 and 555 F1

The 553 F1 was supposed to be an improvement on the 625 F1 but proved itself unreliable and for the time being the factory had to rely on the slower yet dependable 625 which chalked up eight wins in 1954 in a variety of races. A great deal of interchanging of parts between the 625s and 553s gave no improvements and the Mercedes-Benz W196 with their 8-cylinder engine and streamlined bodywork had little difficulty in overcoming the ills which beset the Ferrari team.

For 1955 changes were made to both the 625 and 553, the former now designated 625 A and the latter the 555 Supersqualo. Success, however, was not forthcoming and the only win was in the European Grand Prix held at Monaco in May when Maurice Trintignant drove a 625 A with a 555 engine.

The Lancia-Ferraris

The Lancia D50 was showing some promise in 1955 until the company's dire financial position put paid to any further development work and stopped its competition life. Ferrari was getting nowhere with unreliable and outclassed cars and he had nothing coming along until fortune smiled on him from an unexpected quarter. Arguments over the fate of the Lancia D50s resulted in all the cars, their

The Lancia Ferrarris at Barcelona for the 1954 Spanish GP. Rare color pictures show the rather elementary pit arrangements and Mike Hawthorn at the wheel.

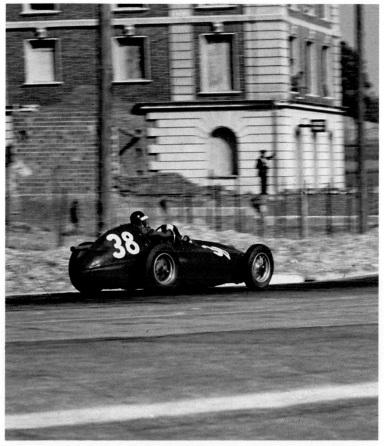

equipment, chief technicians and designer of the D50, Vittorio Jano, transferring to Maranello.

The D50 chassis was a multi-tubular spaceframe with the engine being used as an upper connecting member. Panniers on outriggers held the fuel and were located between the front and rear wheels with an additional small fuel tank in the tail.

The 90 degree V8 engine had a displacement of 2488cc, twin camshafts per bank of cylinders, two valves, two plugs and twin magnetos. Four Solex 40 P11 carburetors fed the fuel and with a compression ratio of 11.9:1 the power output was 250bhp at 8100rpm. Wherever possible, without weakening any part, Jano had drilled holes and the bodywork was aluminum to keep the weight down.

Under the prancing horse insignia the D50s were entered for the Italian Grand Prix over the Monza road-cum-track circuit. Ferrari was contracted to run on Englebert tires which were not only unsuitable for the Lancias but also for the Ferraris over such a circuit. The D50s were withdrawn but the Ferraris ran with Castellotti making 3rd place.

Overwintering at Maranello was an unwieldy collection of cars — outdated 625s, unmanageable and unreliable 555 Supersqualos and four Lancia D50s with suspect handling qualities. And in the meantime Ferrari had Juan Manuel Fangio, World Driver Champion, under contract.

Fangio had a modified car for the 1956 Argentine Grand Prix with work carried out on the suspension, and the outrigged panniers had been mated with sheet metal to the main bodywork. He blew the engine during practice and though he started the race with the car had further mechanical problems so switched to Musso's car which had had only minor modifications. He won at 79.38mph and went on to collect first place in the Buenos Aires City Grand Prix at 83.09mph.

Fangio had quite a reasonable season but owed his 1956 Drivers' Championship to Peter Collins who unselfishly gave up his car to Fangio who went on to win the European Grand Prix at Monza on 2 September. Fangio's car had had problems but Castellotti coaxed it into 8th place.

Further modifications were carried out during the winter to the engine, attention was paid to the suspension and the cars were now designated Ferrari-Lancia 801 and had a power output of 275bhp at 8200rpm.

1957 was not a successful season for the Scuderia, winning some minor events but only taking some placings in the races which counted. However, during the 1956 season Jano had been working on the first of the Dino V6 cars for formula 2 racing. Its first race was the Naples Grand Prix on 28 April where it was entered with two Ferrari-Lancia 801s with all the latest modifications for Collins and Hawthorn. The Dino 156 F2 (as the new car was designated) was in the hands of Musso who had a good race placing the car third behind the two larger capacity 801s.

The Ferrari-Lancias had had their day and perhaps Ferrari was not sorry as the cars had not been designed but only developed by his engineering team. Now the factory could get on, after the hiccup, with designing its own cars once more. After all a Ferrari is a Ferrari and not a Lancia!

The 156 F2, 246 F1, 256 F1 and 296 M1

All the V6 cars and some of the V8s, including one gran turismo (the 308 GT4 2+2 bore the prefix Dino after Ferrari's son for he was mainly responsible for suggesting this configuration.

The first V6 produced by the works was the 156 F2 which Musso drove in the Naples Grand Prix in 1957 where it was placed third. The engine was quite new with the V at an angle of 65 degrees and with the two banks of three cylinders staggered with the left bank slightly ahead of the right bank. The four overhead camshafts, fuel, oil and water pumps were chain driven from the front of the crankshaft. Three twin-choke Weber 42 DCN carburetors were located in the engine V and protruding through the hood were covered by a metal cowl with an air intake. There were two plugs per cylinder sparked by twin magnetos originally driven from the front of the inlet camshafts. Transmission was via a dry multi-plate clutch and 4-speed gearbox in unit with the final drive. Dry sump lubrication was employed. Chassis was a semi-space frame with front suspension of double wishbones of unequal length and coil springs while at the rear the de Dion tube was aft the gearbox with a transverse leaf spring above the final drive unit. Twin radius arms were used at the rear and damping all round was with Houdaille vane-type shock absorbers.

Besides the outing at Naples the car was used in practice by all the drivers at Monaco but was not raced. However, Maurice Trintignant drove the 156 F2 in the Coupe de Vitesse which preceded the Reims Grand Prix on 14 July. After a race-long duel with two Cooper-Climaxes (both finally blew their motors) Trintignant scored its first victory.

For 1958 the 156 F2 had a true spaceframe and appeared twice being posted 2nd by Peter Collins at Reims and 5th at the Nurburgring (in the formula 2 race) by Phil Hill. 1959 produced a 2nd place at Siracusa only. For 1960 the 156 F2

was similar in specification to the formula 1 cars with independent rear suspension (unequal length wishbones and coil springs and the engine angled with the propshaft across the cockpit floor.) A 5-speed gearbox was installed in unit with a redesigned final drive. Two fuel tanks were located on either side of the cockpit forming the sides of the body. The first race was at Siracusa which von Trips won after Moss's Porsche had retired but on 24 July at Solituderennen, von Trips had a rear-engined tipo which he took to a narrow win by 3.6 seconds from Hans Herrmann's Porsche. The same car and driver won the formula 2 category in the Italian Grand Prix at Monza.

The final event in which the formula 2 cars participated was at Modena on 2 October. Richie Ginther had the front-

engined car and took 2nd place while von Trips had to be content with a third. This was the last formula 1 or 2 race in which a front-engined Ferrari took part.

Ferrari had obviously decided that if the formula 2 cars had proved satisfactory he would go on to build 2.5-liters V6 units for 1958. Also for 1958 the FIA was being 'forced' by the petroleum companies to use more or less ordinary pump fuel as they felt that its use in racing would be a sales boost for their products. It was, therefore, decided that 130 octane 'Avgas' aviation fuel would be used from 1958. This was no problem for Ferrari as his formula 2 cars had run on normal fuel so development of the basic unit would be easy while other contenders for the formula 1 crown would have to convert their engines from alcohol-based fuels.

In September 1957 at the Modena Grand Prix Collins and Musso had two formula 2 cars but engines bored out from 1500 to 1860cc. Both cars performed well even if neither won. The next stage was at the Moroccan Grand Prix when two new units were tried out. Hawthorn's had a capacity of 2195cc while Collins had the full-blown engine for 1958 with a displacement of 2417cc. After 10 laps Hawthorn retired with engine trouble and Collins spun twice, on the second occasion damaging the nose too badly to continue.

The front-engined Dino 246 formula 1 had a full season of racing in 1958 starting with the South American events, the Argentine and Buenos Aires Grand Prix, when three cars were available for the first race and a fourth car, which was late in arriving, was available for the second race. Luigi Musso posted two seconds while Hawthorn had a third in the Argentine Grand Prix.

Except in the Dutch and German Grand Prix the 246 F1 had a reasonable, if not good season, winning five races and finishing either second or second and third in the others. For the two last grands prix of the season the 256 F1 made its appearance – von Trips driving one in the Italian Grand Prix at Monza and Mike Hawthorn in the Moroccan race on 19 October using the same car.

A number of modifications were carried out on the formula 1 cars for 1959. Coil spring rear suspension with Koni telescopic dampers was now standard on all cars and by this time Ferrari had been convinced that disk brakes were superior to the drum so Dunlops were fitted. Dunlop tires also replaced the Engleberts. The body received attention from Fantuzzi who gave it a slimmer line with high cockpit sides and a longer tail.

The annual South American races had been cancelled so

The Tasman F2 series cars were the result of installing a Dino 246 engine in a 158 F1 chassis for the 1966 season, but the project was abandoned after John Surtees' accident in Canada the previous September. The cars raced throughout Europe until 1968 and were still taking antipodean honors in 1970.

the season started in Europe with two races in England. The Aintree '200' for formula 1 cars attracted two Ferraris, the revised Dino 246 F1 for Tony Brooks and the 256 F1 (which now developed 300bhp) for Jean Behra. Due to various retirements Behra came out the winner at 88.76mph followed home by Tony Brooks. At Silverstone, for the Daily Express Trophy, Tony Brooks and Phil Hill drove the 246 F1s but only Hill finished and he was fourth. Brooks had a reasonable season winning the European Grand Prix, held at Reims on 5 July and also the German Grand Prix.

Places were obtained in the remaining championship races for 1959 so the season was not quite fruitless although the Dinos could be said to be in decline. It also seemed strange that more use was not made of the 256 F1 which had won at Aintree and was not fielded again during the season.

1960 was the final season for the front-engined formula 1 cars run by the works and their decline was more noticeable, Ferrari gaining a few places but too many retirements due mainly to drive-shaft and other transmission failures.

The day of the rear-engined Ferrari was about to begin, and to start with, in 1961, they did it in style. The first Ferrari formula 1 rear-engined car had made its debut in the Monaco Grand Prix, around the houses, as early as 29 May 1960. The prototype incorporated many features of the existing cars including chassis, suspension etc. but the 246 F1 unit was behind the driver. There was a new 5-speed gearbox and final drive unit with the disk brakes mounted inboard. The clutch was located in the air-stream at the rear of the car. The car had been put together somewhat hurriedly and its handling was not all that could be desired indicating that the factory had a great deal to learn about

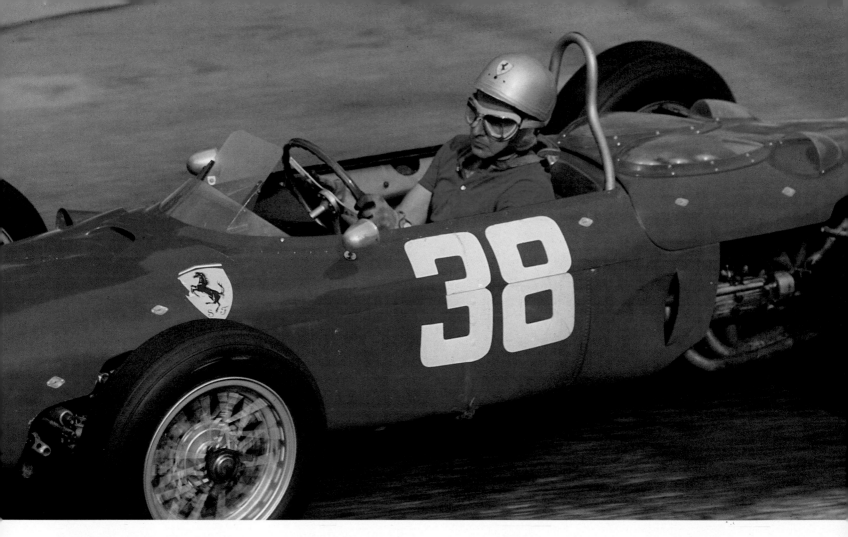

suspension when the engine was rear-mounted. However, even on such a twisting road circuit as Monte Carlo Richie Ginter who had the drive did bring the car home in 6th place.

The Tipo 156 F1

While the front-engined Dino 246 was in its last throes in opposition to the British rear-engined cars during 1960 work had been in progress at Maranello in preparation for the 1.5-liter formula to become effective on 1 January 1961. Carlo Chiti was, in the main, responsible for the design of the 156 F1 and it became an immediate success.

It was often the case that Ferrari refused to be rushed into new innovations – such as disk brakes, rear-mounted engines etc. until he had convinced himself that they were workable. But he was always ready for any new regulations set out by the FIA. For 1961 he would be prepared while the British constructors, who were arguing with the authorities over the new formula, would be left behind as they had convinced themselves that they had a good case for its postponement.

The new Ferrari had a 65 degree V6 unit with four overhead camshafts and had similarities to the Jano V6 formula 2 engine of 1957. A 5-speed gearbox was in unit with the final drive with the clutch assembly at the very rear and the disk brakes inboard. With minor alterations the first car used the chassis of the rear-engined Monaco car (1960) with particular attention being paid to the suspension as the early chassis had shown poor handling qualities. After satisfactory tests at Modena von Trips was sent with the 156 F1 for the 142-mile Solitude Grand Prix on 24 July 1960, which he won from Lotus and Porsche at 102.22mph.

Some minor detailed changes were carried out over the winter and the works had every hope of a good 1961 season with a great line-up of drivers – Phil Hill, Wolfgang von

Trips and Richie Ginther with Willy Mairesse and Ricardo Rodriguez as reserves. The most striking feature of the cars was the shark-like twin-nostril nose which was to be noted also on the sports prototype cars of the time.

The first appearance of the 156 F1 was at Siracuse when a car loaned to the Italian Federation of Scuderias Automobile (a mixture of various Italian racing teams) and driven by Giancarlo Baghetti won the 56 lap race to everyone's surprise. He performed the same feat at Posillipo (Naples Grand Prix) on 14 May!

While changes had been made to the 156 F1 during the winter work was also proceeding on a new lighter version V6 engine. The V had been widened to 120 degrees which improved the overall balance of the engine and at the same time gave a lower center of gravity resulting in a lower body-line. Weber had produced a new twin-choke carburetor for the wide-angled engine, the 40 IF3C, giving a power output of 190bhp at 9500rpm.

The works entered 65 degree cars for Phil Hill and von Trips and a 120 degree car for Richie Ginther at Monaco on 14 May. While Ginther was pushing Moss (Lotus) very hard over the last part of the race he just failed to beat him to the finish line, being 3 seconds behind with Hill third and von Trips fourth. Not a bad beginning. The season progressed with four championship victories for the 120 degree engine and one (the French Grand Prix at Reims) for the 65 degree unit. The Dutch event was a one-two placing while at Spa Francorchamps (Belgian Grand Prix) a clean sweep for all four Ferraris (three 120 degree followed by a 65 degree car). It was fortunate that Hill won the 'home ground' event at Monza as three of the marque cars retired and von Trips was fatally injured on lap 2 when he and Jim Clark collided.

The winter of 1961 was one of dissent and discontent. Chief engineer Carlo Chiti and team manager Tavoni together with other senior staff walked out. No light has

Left: Bandini in his first season with Ferrari at the 1962 Monaco GP.

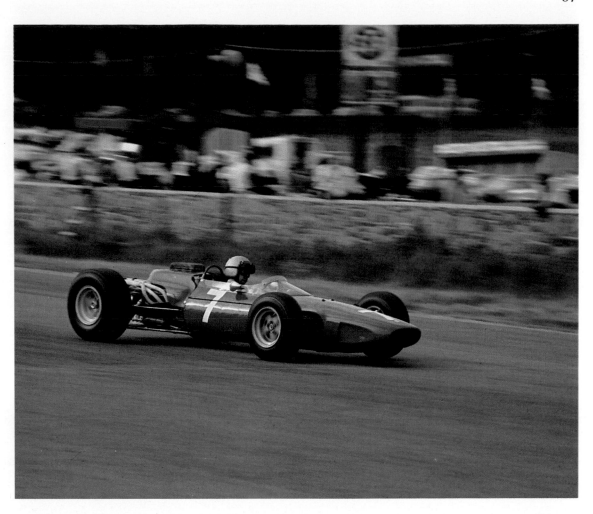

Right: Bandini four years later, this time at the 1966 Belgian GP.

ever been thrown on the row which culminated in this unprecedented happening but it did mean that vital work came to a standstill.

1962 proved a difficult year for the factory as most of the cars were updated 1961 models and the only important development was a 6-speed gearbox and an experimental 65 degree engine with a displacement of 1480cc used by Willy Mairesse for the Brussels Grand Prix. Mairesse was not exactly an exemplary driver, being more of a 'harum scarum' type and lived up to his reputation in the race, spinning off and not being averse to 'knocking off his rivals. He won!

Due to industrial troubles in Italy Ferrari missed the French Grand Prix and also a formula 1 race at Reims but was back for the German Grand Prix at the Nurburgring where one car was new with a multi-tubular chassis built from lighter and smaller diameter tubing. The engine and 6-speed gearbox with the outboard clutch were retained. The frontal area had been greatly reduced by the use of a reclined driving position which meant moving forward the steering box and track rods to give the drivers' feet and pedals more room. Following Lotus practise the chassis members carried water to and from the rear-mounted radiator. The body had been redesigned with slim fuel tanks on either side of the cockpit. The former twin-nostril nose had been abandoned and it was now an oval opening and much shorter. Phil Hill was supposed to have the car but found he slid down too far each time he tried it! So Bandini had the drive, Phil Hill and Baghetti 120 degree cars and Rodriguez a 65 degree model. The new Ferrari did not do well with the older car taking 6th place with Baghetti 10th. Bandini crashed and Hill retired with handling problems.

Generally the Scuderia had a very moderate season including a poor Monza where Ferrari always hopes to do well. Phil Hill had become disenchanted with the cars and

Maranello generally. Never an easy man to deal with he never did understand the Italians nor could he grasp the fact that Ferrari put his cars first and drivers a poor second. After all he must have known the score for he had been driving the sports racing cars before he was promoted to the formula cars. On the other hand the 156 F1 was now passé and very little had been done in the way of any real revision. Anyway he left the Scuderia but Ferrari had his new number one driver already lined up in the person of John Surtees, and one of the very few motorcyclists to succeed on four wheels.

1963 saw a further revision of the 156 F1 with a rear suspension which followed that of the Lotus but this had to be modified after testing. During the winter further development was undertaken and the car for 1963 came out with an even lighter frame and suspension reverting to the 1962 model.

Rumor had it that Ferrari was not only developing a V8 but also a flat 12 engine and by the spring it had become common knowledge. It would be some time before either were ready so the 156 F1 had to do duty but the Webers were now replaced by Bosch high-pressure fuel injection. The 6-speed gearbox was located between the engine and rear axle but was now of a more compact size. The body was redesigned from the one which Bandini had for the German Grand Prix having a longer, tapering nose with a high sloping tail and the fuel intakes covered by gauze. The roll bar was kept low and it is doubtful whether it would have given the driver much protection if the car had overturned.

The season showed the further decline of the 156 F1 120 degree car. Too many retirements due to a variety of ailments and apart from John Surtees winning the German Grand Prix, the Mediterranean event at Pergusa, and the Rand Grand Prix at Kyalami, there wasn't much to shout about. Surtees did post a second and a third and Bandini a second at Kyalami.

The 158 F1

The V6 unit had been well-worked over during the winter and improvements made to the monocoque chassis. At the same time work had been progressing on the new V8 which had undergone tests at Monza in the autumn. Despite this the new car was hastily buttoned-up a few days before it made its debut at the Sicilian event at Siracusa on 12 April. Even the bodywork was a trifle rough by Ferrari standards!

Bandini in the V6 led until Surtees' V8 passed him and stayed ahead until the finish. While chasing Arundell (Lotus) Bandini set a new lap record, passed him on lap 37 and went on to take second place.

The 90 degree V8 had a displacement of 1487cc with twin overhead camshafts per bank of cylinders, twin plugs per cylinder and Bosch high-pressure fuel injection. The power output was 220bhp at 11,000rpm. Unfortunately the V8 failed to live up to its first success at Siracusa until Surtees won the German Grand Prix at Nurburgring on 2 August with a further victory in the Italian Grand Prix (Monza). He did, however, have second places at Solitude, Watkins Glen and the Mexican event at Magdalena Mixhuca. His few victories and reasonable placings brought him the Drivers' World Championship. With the exception of the Italian Grand Prix when Scarfiotti drove a 156 F1 into 10th place and Pedro Rodriguez drove a similar car in the Mexican race the Scuderia ran a two-car team of Surtees and Bandini throughout 1964.

The long-awaited flat 12 car, the 1512 F1, was on hand at Monza for the Italian Grand Prix, but Ferrari decided that insufficient testing had been done so withdrew the car from the race.

After the Italian event the row which had been brewing between Ferrari and the Italian Automobile Club reached a point of no-return – well at least as long as Ferrari wanted it to continue! The furore was over the non-homologation of the 250 LM as a gran turismo car. 100 had to be built before homologation would be granted for it to compete in the GT category otherwise it had to run as a prototype. The row had, of course, started with the FIA. The result was that Ferrari handed in his competition licence and vowed his cars would never race in Italy again!

In view of all this Ferrari asked Luigi Chinetti of NART to enter and run his 158 F1 and 1512 F1 in the United States and Mexican Grand Prix and they were to run in the American racing colors of blue and white. Bandini had the flat 12 for both races, retiring with engine trouble at Watkins Glen and finishing third in the Mexican event.

The 1512 F1

The flat 12 had only two outings in 1964 but ran a full season in 1965 driven mainly by Bandini. The South African Grand Prix was now transferred to early January and two cars (the V8 for Surtees and flat 12 for Bandini) were shipped out to East London. Team manager Eugenio Dragoni was nominated as entrant since Ferrari had not, at that time, re-applied for his entrants' competition licence.

Above: The 1965 season produced a mixed entry for Ferrari F1 cars. This is the 8 cylinder engine at Monaco. Left: Surtees with the car at the Dutch GP.

Right; First showing for the big 12-cylinder engine in the 1512F1 at Monaco in 1965.

Surtees took the V8 to second place but finished a long way behind winner Jim Clark's Lotus. Bandini retired on lap 67.

The 1512 F1 (or 512 F1 as it is also called) had a 180 degree flat 12 engine with a cubic capacity of 1489.6cc. There were two camshafts per bank of cylinders, Lucas fuel injection replaced the Bosch high-pressure unit and ignition was by four coils and distributors. In 1964 there was one plug per cylinder but for 1965 two plugs per cylinder. Compression ratio was 9.8:1 with a power output of 220bhp at 11,500rpm (increased to 225bhp for 1965). Much of the running gear was similar to that of the 158 F1 with the chassis of monocoque structure forming the cockpit and stressed skin compartments for fuel tanks made from riveted sheet steel.

Neither the 158 F1 nor the flat 12 scored a single victory in 1965 although both had reasonable placings in a number of races. After the Italian Grand Prix Surtees took his Lola T70 to the CanAm Canadian Grand Prix where he received terrible injuries when the hub-carrier collapsed during practice. It was thought at the time that he would never race again but he was back again in a racing car by May 1966.

The 312 F1

For 1966 the FIA changed the regulations for formula 1 racing limiting engine capacities to 3-liters unsupercharged or 1500cc supercharged. It was not unexpected when Ferrari declared that his contender would be a V12 unit — after all he had all the experience in the world to produce a reliable and fast engine with this configuration even if the last 'pure' racing engine had been in 1953. Ing. Rocchi was given the job of designing the engine and he chose to base the design on the 4-liter unit which powered the 330 P3.

The 60 degree V12 engine had a displacement of 2989cc and featured twin overhead camshafts per bank of cylinders. Ignition was by two plugs per cylinder with four coils and twin distributors. Lucas fuel injection, similar to the system used by the 1512 F1 fed fuel from a high pressure pump mounted on top of the engine. With a compression ratio of 11.8:1 the power output was 360bhp at 10,000rpm.

Only one of the new models was ready for the season's first race at Siracusa on 1 May with Surtees at the wheel, who duly won. As make-weight Ferrari sent along a Dino V6 which had been prepared for Surtees to use in the Tasman races during the European winter months but Surtees' severe injuries precluded his participation. This car had a 1965 formula 1 V8 chassis with a 2417cc engine and driven by Bandini took second place.

1966 was not all that satisfactory with only two more victories in championship races. John Surtees won at Spa Francorchamps and Scarfiotti won at Monza followed home by Mike Parkes. After the Spa race Surtees was part of the team for the annual Le Mans race but Dragoni, team manager, considered he might not be sufficiently fit for all his stints during the endurance race and brought in Scarfiotti as spare driver. Upset, Surtees walked out and took off for Maranello to see Enzo Ferrari but got no change from him and Surtees left the Scuderia for good. Dragoni never was blessed with tact!

The young New Zealander, Chris Amon, was signed up for 1967 but was unable to take his seat for the Race of Champions at Brands Hatch on 12 March being injured in an accident on the way to the circuit. Bandini took his place in the latest car which now had the exhausts, in an asbestos trough, inside the engine V. Scarfiotti had a normal 1966 model and finished 5th while Bandini made second place.

The Daily Express Trophy at Silverstone was won by Mike Parkes and the only other victory during the season was at Siracusa when Parkes and Scarfiotti with little in the way of opposition toured the circuit and crossed the finish line together to score a dead-heat and a rather hollow victory.

Bandini and Amon were sent to Monaco for the Monte Carlo Grand Prix. On lap 71 the two Ferraris were running second and third but on lap 82 Bandini misjudged a chicane, struck a barrier and the car, out of control, hit the outside straw bales and losing a wheel overturned in the road. The car was righted but suddenly the fuel tank exploded trapping the strapped-in Bandini. He died of severe burns. His death left a great gap in the Ferrari set-up as he was not only a first rate driver but popular at the works and amongst the Italian enthusiasts.

Three cars were entered for the Belgian Grand Prix for Amon, Parkes and Scarfiotti but they must have felt like many of the other drivers — what chance had they against the sensational new Lotus 49 powered by the V8 Cosworth engine financed by Ford? These cars had made their debut at the Dutch Grand Prix on 4 June. It is interesting to recall that it was at Spa Francorchamps (Belgian GP) that both Brabhams and Ferraris featured the high-mounted rear aerofoils which were to become regular 'wear' on all racing cars for a number of years until they became an integral part of the cars. During the Belgian race Parkes overdid it at the fast left-hander at Blanchimont crashing heavily. This seemed to have unnerved both Amon and Scarfiotti and the latter, having seen a number of his former team mates killed, decided to quit formula 1 racing. This left Chris Amon to see out the remainder of the season as sole Ferrari representative. A heavy and lonely burden especially as the car was not fully competitive but at least it was pretty reliable. So, for Ferrari there was little to rejoice over during 1967 even though a new V12 engine with four valves per cylinder was produced for the Italian Grand Prix at Monza. Amon could only manage 7th place. Ironically the man who had been discarded by Dragoni a year earlier won the race for Honda — none other than John Surtees!

Jacky Ickx joined Amon for the 1968 season with a little help at the season's end from Englishman Derek Bell and in the first race at Kyalami from de Adamich. Once again reliability was the keynote but it doesn't necessarily win races. Ickx did win the French Grand Prix over the Rouen-les-Essarts circuit on 7 July but otherwise he and Chris Amon had to be content with the minor placings.

Late in the season the cylinder heads and camshafts were modified and the cars were now pushing 412bhp at 10,500rpm but for all this Amon retired at the Canadian event on 22 September. The United States Grand Prix saw Bell and Amon retiring while a similar situation prevailed at the Mexican Grand Prix — Amon had transmission failure and Ickx engine failure.

Jacky Ickx couldn't see any furtherance in his career by remaining with Ferrari for 1969 so he left to drive for Brabham but he would be back the following year when an entirely new car would be available. So, once more Amon had to play a solo part driving his last race for Ferrari in the British Grand Prix when he retired with gearbox problems. For the remainder of the season Pedro Rodriguez drove the 312 F1 V12 but without any luck.

Before the 1969 Italian Grand Prix (Monza) on 7 September it became known that a new Ferrari flat 12 grand prix contender was being tested. It was hoped that it would make its debut in the race but in testing at Modena the engine

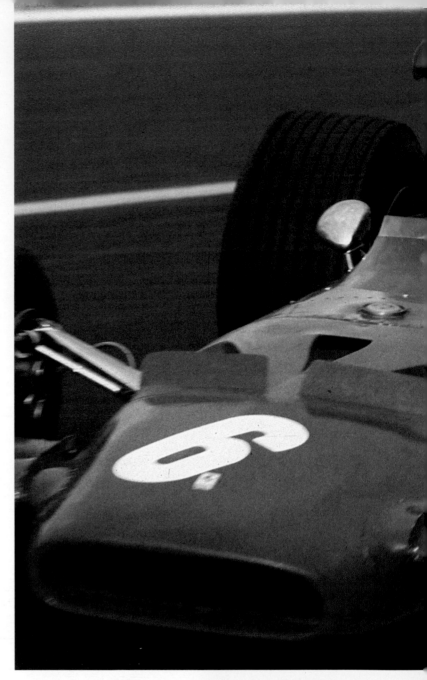

Above: Chris Amon drives the 312F1V12 in the French GP of 1969.

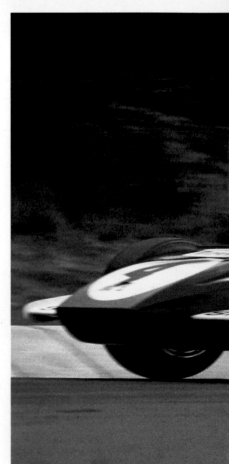

Above right: Jackie Ickx and his 312BF1 at the British Grand Prix in 1971, and Ickx again (right) in the later 312B2F1.

broke. While there were still three more championship events to be run all were overseas and Ferrari was hardly likely to send a brand new car too far from home in the initial stages so its first race appearance was left until 1970.

The 312 B F1

The power unit of the new 312 B owed its origin to the 1965 1512 F1 (which was never fully developed) and the 2-liter flat 12 of the 212 E 'Montagna' sports car with which Peter Schetty won the 1969 European Hill Climb Championship. The flat 12 unit was mounted ahead of and drove the rear wheels. Displacement was 2991cc. The crankcase and cylinder blocks were aluminum alloy and the twin overhead camshafts per bank of cylinders were gear driven, operating two exhaust and two inlet valves. A single plug was ignited by a Marelli transistor and fuel fed by Lucas injection. Compression ratio at 11.8:1 gave a power output of 455bhp at 11,500rpm. Transmission was via a dry multi-plate clutch between the engine and 5-speed gearbox which was in unit with the final drive.

Ickx now back with Ferrari found he was the only driver for the South African Grand Prix where he retired with a loss of oil. He was also on his own at Jarama for the Spanish event where he crashed and also at Monte Carlo (Monaco GP) where he had drive-shaft failure. Not a good beginning! Things were to improve.

At Spa Francorchamps (Belgian GP) Giunti joined Ickx but the breakthrough did not happen until the Austrian Grand Prix at Osterreichring on 16 August which Ickx won at 129.27mph, followed home by Clay Regazzoni (now a regular team member) with Giunti 7th. This was followed by Regazzoni's win in the Italian Grand Prix at 147.07mph although Ickx and Giunti retired with engine and transmission troubles respectively. Finally, in the Mexican Grand Prix, Ferrari scored a one-two for the second time in the season. So a poor start finished in a total vindication of the new model.

After the euphoria of the 1970 end-of-season races it was not surprising that 1971 also started on a high note with victories in the first three races entered and a 2nd in the Spanish Grand Prix. This was followed by Ickx winning the Jochen Rindt Gedachtnis-Rennen at Hockenheim on 13

June. By the time of the Dutch event Ickx and Regazzoni had the revised semi-monocoque cars with new bodywork — the 312 B2. Ickx won with Regazzoni 3rd. The remainder of the season would best be forgotten for the 312 B2 suffered mainly from engine failure although reliability was again found for the Canadian Grand Prix even if two cars finished down the line while Regazzoni crashed.

For 1972 the 312 B2 power output was boosted to 480bhp at 12,500rpm. Unfortunately all the work carried out was fruitless with only a single victory at the Nurburgring on 30 July with Ickx leading Regazzoni home and Merzario in 12th place.

Early in 1973 the 312 B3 was ready with a full monocoque chassis and side-mounted radiators ahead of the rear wheels which was later changed to a single front-mounted radiator in the nose. Then later in the season the monocoque was revised with the radiators located behind the front wheels. A high air scoop was added behind the driver.

It seemed that after the initial appearance of the 3-liter 312 B3 nothing would go right and 1973 was no better than the previous season. Generally speaking there was reliability but speed and handling were lacking.

1974 saw the return of Regazzoni to the team and the signing of Niki Lauda, an Austrian — it was a reasonably fruitful time and the partnership lasted four years. A new team manager was appointed, Luca Montezemolo, a law student aged 25 who had had some experience with the Lancia Rally Team. It was his job — and he did it well — to combine all the elements of the racing team into a coherent unit and he alone would be responsible for reporting back to Enzo Ferrari. During the winter of 1973 some intensive work was carried out on the 312 B3. The driving seat was moved forward and an additional fuel tank placed between the seat and engine which put more weight on the front. Alterations were made to the front airfoil and a variety of rear airfoils were available for the season, as different types were required depending on the race circuit. In fact a real touch of professionalism had now crept into the organization, something which had been lacking for many years.

The first championship race of the season was the Buenos Aires City Grand Prix and while not in the winner's enclosure Lauda, in his first Ferrari race, posted a second

Left: The engine of the 312T pictured before the 1975 Belgian GP.

Right: Lauda in the 312T2F1 at the Belgian GP just prior to the accident which was expected to end his racing career.

with Regazzoni third. Two weeks later at Interlagos Regazzoni went one better and came second. Lauda retired on lap 2 with a broken wing. The most promising race during the first half of the season was at Jarama for the Spanish event which was a one-two result with Lauda winning, followed home by Regazzoni. Another one-two was posted at Zandvoort, Lauda taking the chequered flag. Lauda also took a 2nd at Dijon for the French Grand Prix with Regazzoni in attendance third.

Regazzoni won at the Nurburgring, Lauda having an accident before completing a lap. The rest of the season was not so successful but on the whole Ferrari must have been quite pleased.

The 312 B3 was still used early in the 1975 season for the South American races and while both drivers scored championship points their placings were low.

The 312 T F1

By the time the South African Grand Prix came round on 1 March 1975 both drivers had the new 312 T although a 312 B3 was also shipped out. Its debut was not spectacular with Lauda doing no better than 5th and Regazzoni having to retire on lap 71 with a broken throttle linkage.

However, before the next championship round Lauda was at Silverstone for a non-championship race which he won.

After all the traumas during the development of the 312 B3 Ferrari was to strike gold with the 312 T. It had a completely new monocoque chassis but more importantly it had a transverse 5-speed gearbox developed for the new car. The letter 'T' after 312 stood for transversale. While this new layout gave a better weight distribution it also gave an efficient power flow alleged to be far in excess of the normal type transmission. This was shown by the power output which was 500bhp at 12,000rpm.

The whole concept of the body was concentrated on its aerodynamic shape giving a better airflow both over and beneath the body.

After the South African Grand Prix and the minor Silverstone race the European season started in earnest at Barcelona on 27 April with the Spanish event. A number of drivers had decided to forgo the race protesting that the

safety precautions were inadequate. Lauda and Regazzoni started qualifying one-two on the grid. Andretti's Parnelli clouted Regazzoni's car on lap 1 knocking it into Lauda's 312 T. Lauda had to retire and Regazzoni went out on lap 11.

The Monaco, Zolder and Anderstorp races were next on the calendar and Niki Lauda was first over the finishing line in all three giving him a good lead in the Drivers' Championship which he was not to lose.

At Zandvoort Lauda failed to catch James Hunt (Hesketh) by one second but reversed the placing at the Paul Ricard circuit. A multiple pile-up at Silverstone resulted in half the 26 field being eliminated but although both Ferraris finished no points were scored.

Lauda should have won the German Grand Prix at the Nurburgring. A front tire puncture about half-way round the long circuit meant he had to get back to his pit on the wheel rim for a change of wheel. However, he scored a further four points for coming in third and once again the irrepressible Regazzoni set a lap record before falling oil pressure led to his motor blowing up. A really wet Austrian Grand Prix over the Osterreichring saw Lauda, who had started on pole, leading for 15 laps but his suspension, as set, could not stand up to the almost awash track, allowing other cars to overtake him. The race was stopped around the halfway mark and with a shortened race distance the 'points finishers' only got half their normal marks!

At the non-championship Swiss Grand Prix (held on the Dijon circuit as the Swiss do not approve of motor racing in their country), Regazzoni won the race with ease.

Ferrari has always tried to make Monza his set piece and loud and long are the wails of the partisan Italian fans and national press if the performance of his cars do not come up to their expectations. As the season had so far shown, the 312 T was the car to beat and it was an hysterical crowd who came to watch as Lauda and Regazzoni were side-by-side at the front of the grid. Regazzoni led from start to finish with Lauda following him for 45 of the 52 laps when a rear shock absorber let him down and Fittipaldi moved up into second place. Lauda, however, hung on to 3rd place and clinched the Drivers' title. Regazzoni also set the fastest lap of the meeting for Ferrari.

To end an excellent season Lauda won the USA Grand

Prix at Watkins Glen, so the factory won the Manufacturers' championship as well, having scored six victories in 14 championship races, plus two non-championship wins.

Ferrari unveiled the 312 T2 in October 1975 but it showed few changes from the original 312 T apart from a slightly shorter wheelbase. The revised car also had to conform with two new regulations. Wing dimensions were limited and the tall, ungainly looking airboxes were taboo. These edicts had to be complied with as from the Spanish GP.

For 1976 the 312 T did good service until the newer car made its debut at Jarama on 2 May for the Spanish event. Lauda had won at Interlagos and Kyalami and Regazzoni had led from start to finish at Long Beach!

The 312 T2s looked a much neater job with the removal of the high airscoops. There were now two NACA-type scoops ahead of and on either side of the windshield which ducted air along the sides of the cockpit to the two boxes of six fuel-injection trumpets.

Lauda could only post a second at Jarama but a dispute over the wing width of James Hunt's winning McLaren promoted Lauda to first (to be reversed a little later). Everything seemed to be going Ferrari's way again but the winning streak began to falter at Anderstorp (Lauda was 3rd) and although finishing 2nd at Brands Hatch Lauda was promoted to first as James Hunt's McLaren had been worked

on during the interval between the stopping of the race (a first lap accident) and its re-start. This, of course, led to the usual protest. In fact disputes on a variety of matters were now creeping into the grand prix scene and over the years have brought motor racing at the top level into disrepute, with 'cheating' being quite common, albeit that the 'cheating' has crept in due to the interpretation constructors have placed on some of the more loosely worded regulations, and if there are loop-holes then those in authority are to be blamed.

All that is as may be after a near-fatality occurred at the Nurburgring on 1 August when Lauda crashed on lap 2. There can be little doubt that the ghastly accident was due to lack of tire adhesion. The circuit was both wet and dry and Lauda was on slicks. The car caught fire and it was only due to the combined efforts of drivers such as Lunger, Edwards, Ertl and Merzario that he was pulled clear of the raging inferno. Given a 50/50 chance of living Lauda finally survived and it says much for his will power that he was back driving a Ferrari in the Italian Grand Prix some six weeks later!

No doubt shocked by the accident the factory did not prepare a car for Regazzoni for the Austrian event. Since Lauda was recovering the lack of an entry didn't really make much sense. With Lauda out of action and Ferrari no

Above: Giles Villeneuve with 312T3F1 at the Monaco circuit for the 1978 GP.

Left: Clay Reggazoni with 312T2F1.

doubt thinking he wouldn't race again during the season, he decided to put Carlos Reutemann (who had left the Brabham outfit) under contract. However, Lauda was ready for the Monza race so three cars were fielded. Lauda took 4th place while Regazzoni was second to Peterson's March.

With Lauda's recovery and the signing of Reutemann Ferrari made an extremely unpopular move — he discarded Regazzoni for 1977. Regazzoni was always popular not only among his fellow drivers but with the Italian fans and press.

With the circus moving over to the North American continent Ferrari had no answer to James Hunt who won both the Mosport (Canadian) and Watkins Glen (USA) events which left Lauda three points ahead of Hunt (68–65) before the final grand prix at Fuji (for the Japanese GP). The race was another fiasco (too many races had turned out to be a travesty of what motor racing should be about during the season). At Fuji visibility was almost nil due to the really appalling weather. It was not really surprising when Lauda decided to call it a day having completed two laps. After all he had had a traumatic season. As Hunt took third place scoring 4 points he pipped Lauda by one point to win the Drivers' championship.

1976 was not a season when anyone could be proud with all the stupid quibbling that had accompanied so many of the events. In fact it was grand prix racing at its worst!

Ferrari, quite naturally, had not been overpleased at Lauda's retirement at Fuji and there can be little doubt that this caused the somewhat brittle and delicate relationship between the two men to break into open conflict before the end of the 1977 season.

All kinds of minor adjustments were made over the winter and during the new season, including moving the driver to a more forward position, revised air intakes and redesigned rear wing mount.

Reutemann and Lauda formed the team up to and including the USA race at Watkins Glen when Lauda decided that he had had enough of going round in circles. His relationship with Ferrari and the factory had reached a new low and it was not until he failed to practice for the Canadian event at Mosport that the motor racing world knew he had quit and agreed to drive for Brabham. Ferrari was, of course, prepared and brought in young Gilles Villeneuve to partner Carlos Reutemann at Mosport where he was awarded 12th place although not running at the finish. At Fuji he had an accident on lap 5 and retired.

Lauda, before leaving the Scuderia, had enjoyed a reasonable season with three championship victories and a number of high placings which enabled him to win back the Drivers' title which he had so narrowly lost the previous season.

The early 1978 races were, as usual, held in South America and while Villeneuve did put in the fastest lap at Buenos Aires he could only finish 8th to Reutemann's 7th. At Rio Reutemann won and so ended the life of the 312 T2 to be replaced at Kyalami (South African GP) by the 312 T3. Both drivers retired on lap 55.

Although the 312 T3 was very different from its predecessor it had many of the details which had been tested out on the 1977 cars but visually the difference was apparent.

The wheelbase was adjustable from 2560 to 2700mm by using various sets of front A-arms. Its track dimensions were also the widest of any of the cars yet built — front 1620mm, rear 1585mm.

1978 was a moderate season for the factory although the new car made first place on four occasions — at the West

Coast Grand Prix won by Reutemann, the British Grand Prix also won by Reutemann, the USA event (Reutemann again) and on his home ground at Montreal in the Canadian GP Gilles Villeneuve achieved his first championship win.

There can be no doubt that the 312 T3 was a reliable car and its performances during the 1978 season were in the main spoiled by the poor quality of the Michelin tires which just could not stand the pace. In spite of this it is doubtful whether the T3 could have withstood the assault of the Lotus 79 which, when on form, was certainly devastating.

Reutemann left the Scuderia at the end of 1978 and was replaced by South African Jody Scheckter. Reutemann had served his term well with the team but perhaps he was too much of a loner; caution was a word which would have best described him. He was not a pursuer, especially if he felt any situation was more or less hopeless!

As for several years past Ferrari relied on his previous season's model to set the scene in South America for 1979. The 312 T3 failed to produce at either track although Villeneuve was 5th and Scheckter 6th in Brazil. In its final appearance Villeneuve won a non-championship race at Brands Hatch.

It was no less a person than Enzo Ferrari himself who described the 312 T4 as the ugliest formula 1 car ever produced by the factory. It was the first Ferrari designed as a wing car and like its contemporaries was slab-sided with a skirted mid-section. Somehow the front wing seemed out on a limb having nothing to do with the rest of the body-work.

Ugly or handsome the T4 showed its paces to good effect at both Kyalami on 3 March and Long Beach (USA) on 8 April when Villeneuve and Scheckter posted a one-two in each race and in that order.

Scheckter then showed his form by winning at Zolder and Monaco and with a reliable car managed to take the Drivers' Championship by winning at Monza on 9 September with team mate Villeneuve following him home.

The 312 T4 rounded off its career at Watkins Glen when Gilles Villeneuve won the USA Grand Prix after finishing in second place on his home ground at Montreal.

The V6 Turbocharged 126 C

Often at Maranello an entirely new concept got 99 per cent attention and the current model given scant attention. By 1980 Ferrari was finished with the boxer configuration for racing and his weight was behind the V6 turbocharged 126 C which would be the 1981 contender from the factory.

The turbo-supercharger has been in evidence for a greater part of the twentieth century and it became generally known as the shortened 'turbocharger'. Its popularity, if it may be so called, has latterly been pioneered by Porsche who used such cars in the CanAm series to great effect.

Ferrari had obviously been keeping a wary eye on the performances of the Renault turbocharged formula 1 cars, noting their strengths and weaknesses and as in earlier years played a wait and see game before his engineering team had mastered the technique so that his cars would be an improvement on the Renaults.

It was in 1978 that the factory looked at the possibility of producing a 1.5-liter turbocharged engine and by 1979 a detailed design for a 120 degree V6 unit had been decided upon. In June 1980 the new car, designated 126 C, was shown to the press. The twin overhead camshafts per bank of cylinders were gear-driven and operated two intake and two exhaust valves per cylinder; with a KKK turbocharger, Lucas fuel injection and the one plug per cylinder was sparked by a Marelli transistor. The power output was 540bhp at 11,000rpm. The aluminum monocoque chassis with fiberglass body panels had side fairings which gave aerodynamic downforce, with sliding skirts.

The front suspension had upper rocker arms with inboard shock absorber units and coil springs. There were wide-based lower A-arms and an anti-roll bar. At the rear the half-shafts had constant velocity joints, upper rocker arms and inboard shock absorber units with coil springs, lower links and anti-roll bar.

Apart from the KKK turbocharger, the Comprex (pressure-exchange system) was also tried out as it gave as much power as the KKK but importantly gave reduced throttle-lag, always a problem in the early days.

At the end of 1980 the future of formula one racing was in a state of flux. Goodyear had pulled out, leaving a number of teams looking for new tires and the FISA/FOCA conflict was still unresolved and at one time it seemed that each side would try to organize its own series of races. FOCA reached an agreement at the Ferrari works on 19 January (the Maranello Agreement) which then had to be approved by the sporting authorities at FISA. The so-called Concorde Agreement was signed by both parties in Paris on 4 March. A somewhat uneasy settlement had been reached.

Due to all this nonsense the South African Grand Prix (which couldn't be postponed from its original date – 7 February) took place without the FISA-faithful teams such as Ferrari and the result was not recognized as a qualifying event by the FISA.

The San Marino race at Imola was elevated to championship status for 1981 and Villeneuve had a new car with an extended wheelbase lengthened by the insertion of a 5-inch spacer in the shape of an aluminum casting between the engine and gearbox – the bodywork being suitably lengthened. The scrutineers had a field day sticking rigidly to the rule book. Out went hydro-pneumatic suspensions, flexible skirts and flexible strips used to bridge the gap between sidepods and rear wheels! Just about every car, including the Ferraris, was illegal in one way or another. The usual pit lane politicians had a wonderful time. However, a compromise was reached – hydro-pneumatic systems could stay but skirts had to be made of rigid material!

Both cars proved their reliability but that was all.

Two weeks later at Zolder for the Belgian Grand Prix the cheating on skirts was carried to further lengths. Most teams had by now equipped their cars with adjustable ride height systems and FISA had clarified the 6 centimeter rule which was naturally ignored by all. The cheat was to have cockpit control of the ride height – so on entering the pit area the ride height was in the 'up' legal position but once on the circuit in the 'down' position. During the race the Ferraris still showed their reliability but handling was the main problem – in fact the cars required a chassis man but attention to handling and the proper setting up of the cars was still some way off. It was during the 1980 season that the Ferraris acquired the somewhat insulting but nevertheless warranted name of 'moving chicanes'!

After the Monaco race the factory announced that Dr Harvey Postlethwaite would be joining the design team which must, at least, have put some heart into Ferrari supporters who were seeing an excellent design being wasted through atrocious handling. What point in a fast, reliable engine if it won't go where it's directed?

The 126 C2

In November Ferrari announced that for 1982 his cars would run on Goodyear tires. It had seemed to him that the Michelin company had been favoring the Renault team at his expense. Work had also been progressing on the revised car which had a new suspension, new bodywork and a narrower gearbox. The chassis was a slim monocoque constructed in an aluminum-skinned honeycomb material with carbon fiber used for the front and rear bulkheads, the main structure being bonded together with a complete absence of rivets. It was hard to believe that the under-the-skin structure was indeed Ferrari! The engine and twin KKK turbo installation had been tidied up and with further development of the V6 unit the power claimed was 580bhp. The wheelbase had been shortened, the track widened and with a paring in weight it neared the legal minimum of 580kg.

Pironi was sent out to Kyalami with the much modified 126 C which was, in fact, the prototype for the 126 C2. For the last two days of testing two of the new 126 C2s arrived. The first day of testing did not materialize as the drivers took 'industrial action' objecting to the small print on their licences. The trouble was resolved temporarily but serious practice was left to one day. Various problems arose with the new cars and during the race Villeneuve suffered a broken turbo and Pironi struggled through to 18th place completing only 71 of the 77 laps.

After the South African event all appeared sweetness as it seemed that FOCA supremo Bernie Ecclestone and FISA boss Balestre were now the best of chums, but Ecclestone and Enzo Ferrari were at war, with acrimonious letters flying around.

The Argentine Grand Prix scheduled for 7 March was cancelled. For the Brazilian event Villeneuve had a new car with modified bodywork as the front fairings were now blended into the sidepods. Villeneuve left the field standing at the start but an error on lap 30 put him out of contention. Pironi was 8th. A new cheating device was thought up for the race by the Brabham and Williams teams. This consisted of a large plastic water bottle filled before scrutineering so as to ensure the car was the legal minimum weight of 580kg before the race but jettisoned during the early laps so as to reduce this weight. The 'war' was still on! Both Ferrari and Renault lodged protests.

The circus next moved to Long Beach where further protests were in evidence. Pironi's Ferrari appeared on the second day of practice with a peculiar looking rear wing consisting of two staggered narrow chord wings with a central mounting. The whole wing was as wide as the car and was meant to be Ferrari's challenge to the so-called 'water-cooled' brakes. Both cars were fitted with the new wings and also had nose wings for the first time. Villeneuve came

in 3rd but Ken Tyrrell protested against the new rear wings and was upheld by the same stewards who had passed the new device in pre-race scrutineering. So the farce of protest and counter-protest proceeded.

The San Marino Grand Prix (at Imola) on 25 April was the first European event and to everyone's surprise Enzo Ferrari turned up for pre-race testing. A week previously the FIA Court of Appeal decreed that the 'water-bottle' ploy was illegal and all cars finishing a race had to comply with the minimum legal weight of 580kg. They also disqualified Piquet and Rosberg from their Brazilian places over the 'water-cooled' brakes protest. Predictably the FOCA reacted in a childish manner and boycotted the race with the exception of Mr Tyrrell and his equipe (he ran his cars under his Italian sponsors' banner) and also the ATS team. The FISA boys (Ferrari, Renault and Alfa) contested the race and the organizers managed to get a grid of 14 cars. At least it would be a straight fight between Renault and Ferrari which the latter won with a one-two placing.

Zolder for the Belgian Grand Prix was next but when Villeneuve went out to improve his grid position on the last practice session he was killed in a horrifying accident. A lonely Didier Pironi went to Monaco and with a number of the early leaders falling by the wayside found himself in the lead. However, on the final lap he ceased to motor and was awarded second place.

After Monaco it was announced that Frenchman Patrick

The British Grand Prix in 1979. Whatever Enzo Ferrari may have thought of the 312T4 there is an old saying that beauty is only skin deep.

Tambay, a very experienced and first rate formula 1 driver, would join Ferrari.

All the teams flew the Atlantic again to meet up in Detroit for the latest grand prix circuit laid out on 2.59 miles of public roads surrounding the Renaissance Center where Pironi made it to the finish line in third place. This event was followed by the Canadian Grand Prix where Pironi was still on his own and was unfortunate to stall on the grid. Ricardo Paletti (Osella) came storming up and hit the Ferrari's rear and succumbed to his injuries. The race was held up and restarted somewhat late. Pironi had to use the spare car which had not been set-up and could only finish in 9th place.

Both Pironi and Tambay did well at Brands Hatch finishing 2nd and 3rd respectively with Niki Lauda well ahead of the field and quite uncatchable. The French Grand Prix at Paul Ricard was somewhat boring with the two Renaults well in control followed by Pironi and Tambay. For the second time in the season tragedy hit the Ferrari team. During the last practice session for the German Grand Prix at Hockenheimring Pironi hit Alain Prost's Renault suffering severe injuries, but fortunately his recovery is now assured. In the race Tambay was on his own and driving well was in second place by quarter-distance. By lap 19 he inherited first place when the leader, Piquet (Brabham), made a stupid error. Tambay just drove on to give Ferrari another win.

Ferrari as always wanted to do well before the 'home crowd' at Monza for the Italian Grand Prix on 12 September so it was necessary to field a complete team of two cars. Good drivers not already under contract were not available — at least those who could handle formula 1 cars, so he had to go outside the current circus pilots. Andretti was an obvious choice; he had been under contract to the Scuderia in the past and had recent formula 1 experience. Although under contract to drive in USAC events he was free for the Monza weekend and with Tambay would make a strong team. Although the 126 C2 did not win it made a strong bid for victory and Tambay crossed the finish line second with Andretti third.

The season's final event was at Las Vegas, hardly a grand prix circuit, more like a scaleletrix course which should be eliminated from the annual championship. Although Andretti had a USAC event it was possible for him to take in the Las Vegas event but he might as well have stayed away. The 126 C2 was not handling too well and Andretti got all crossed up at a right-hander and found himself in the sand unable to extract his car.

With all the year's traumas the 126 C2 had acquitted itself well and although it is always dangerous to speculate where motor racing is concerned the thought remains — if either Villeneuve had lived or Pironi had not been sidelined would one or the other have emerged as world drivers' champion?

Designed and built by Pininfarina, the 365 GTC/4 was shown on the Ferrari stand at the 1971 Paris Salon and, apart from the 400 saloons, was the last of the V12 engined cars.

GT road cars

The Gran Turismo cars up to 3 liters

There have been few automobile manufacturers who started out by building cars which they raced successfully and from the knowledge gained went on to construct fast and elegant road cars. It is a path not to be recommended unless the constructor has immense faith in himself and, of course, his product.

Ettore Bugatti showed the way, starting around the year 1911, to be followed by Enzo Ferrari after the second world war and the other name which comes readily to mind is Colin Chapman. Many more have made it the other way round.

Ferrari's beginnings are well chronicled and his early Colombo designed V12 unit was devized with three purposes in mind – an engine for a racing car, a sports car and a road car even if in the early days the comforts of the latter for touring were somewhat inadequate in interior design.

The 166 Series

First of the road cars was the 166 Sport but few of these were built and a brochure of the period had a line drawing of a notchback coupe with some provision for back-seat passengers! Touring, it would seem, was the designer and builder of the bodywork.

The V12 engine had a single overhead camshaft per bank of cylinders, a single plug and two distributors. Three Weber 32 DCF carburetors fed the fuel, and transmission was via a 5-speed gearbox mated to the engine. Suspension was the usual independent double wishbones with a transverse spring at the front and the rigid axle and semi-elliptic springs at the rear. With a compression ratio of 7.5:1 the power output was 110bhp at 6000rpm.

The 195 Series

Ferrari continued with his usual process when introducing the 195 by enlarging the bore to give a capacity of 2431cc. There were two models – the Sport and the Inter (the road-going car) with a probable production of near 20. While the Sport had three Weber 32 DCF carburetors, the Inter had a single carburetor of the same type and the wheelbase was longer at 2500mm. The power output was 130bhp at 6000rpm.

The 250 Series

It was with this series that Ferrari finally established himself as the manufacturer of high class gran turismo cars. Up to 1953 the works had built a moderate number of cars — about 200 all told. By the time the 250 Series went out of production with the 1964 GTO the figure had risen to between 3000 and 3500. However, the rapid increase was not due solely to the 250s as other models had also been produced in the intervening years.

The 250 Series saw the light of day in March 1952 when a Vignale bodied berlinetta powered by an experimental 3-liter engine was driven out of the factory gates for its first run. As with other models the series was produced in three versions — competition berlinettas, sports cars and gran turismo cars.

At the Paris Salon in 1953 Ferrari had two new gran turismo cars on show with differing engine capacities but using a common chassis. The smaller 3-liter tipo 250 Europa was the first of the touring 250 Series and the V12 engine was from the Lampredi long block range. They are, at times, referred to as the 'first series Europa' and their production run was short, some 20 examples being built. Most were coupes bodied by Pinin Farina who also built a spyder body on one chassis. Vignale did the coachwork on two chassis.

The 2963cc engine had a single camshaft per bank of cylinders, a single plug, coil ignition and three Weber 36 DCF carburetors. The 4-speed gearbox was in unit with the engine. The power output was 200bhp at 6000rpm.

By late 1954 Ferrari had returned to the Colombo-based V12 unit and with the 250 Europa GT started a long and profitable line of 3-liter 250s. At that time GT racing was about to replace the sports cars so homologation of the series was obtained which led finally to Ferrari's great success in this type of competition.

At the 1956 Geneva show, using the chassis and the

Right: The 195S used an enlarged Tipo 166 engine and was clothed in classic bodywork by Carrozzeria Touring and was also built with spyder bodies.

Below: The Tipo 166 appeared in 1948 as an uprated Tipo 159, which in turn was a bored-out Tipo 125, the first car to appear under Ferrari's own name.
Bottom left and right: The Tipo 166 Corsa Spyder dates from 1948 and uses that enlarged 1995cc V12 engine.

engine of the 250 Europa GT, Pinin Farina produced a coupe version and it was intended that the firm would build the coachwork. A few prototypes were produced but in the final analysis some 70 plus of the cars were completed by Carrozzeria Boano. These cars became known as the 'low roof coupes'. By 1957 Carrozzeria Boano had become Carrozzeria Ellena. The new firm produced about 50 bodies on the Ferrari chassis with a higher roof line and called them the 'high roof coupes' to distinguish the styling of the two versions. The body side panels were flat and the bumpers were not for protection but show. Many of the minor components, such as door latches, handles etc. were standard fittings from either the Fiat or Alfa Romeo factories. Up to that time it could be said that these coupes were the most comfortable Ferraris built. Surprisingly neither Boano nor Ellena identified their handiwork on the coachwork.

Pinin Farina had been working during the winter of 1957/1958 on a new style coupe for the 250 Series. The first car was shown in June 1958 and production was carried through until 1960 by which time 350 models of the 250 GT Pinin Farina coupes had been built. There had been some changes to the V12 engine during this period. Disk brakes were an optional extra but later became standard when Ferrari was convinced of their superiority over the drum brake.

Going back to the 1956 Geneva show the Ferrari stand had on display a Boano built cabriolet but at that time the project was dropped and it was left to Pinin Farina to design the finished car. It was not the first 'open' Ferrari as some had been built earlier but it was the first of a series. Altogether four prototypes were produced before the production model was to be seen at the 1957 Paris Salon. It was a classic of its kind and some 40 were built in the first series.

Besides the cabriolet Pinin Farina designed a second open car, the 250 GT California spyder, bodywork on which was carried out by Scaglietti. Pinin Farina, who was, by now, the main designer for Ferrari, was into the Series II cabriolets by 1959 and by 1962 when they were phased out, a total of around 210 had been built.

All these cars were two-seaters and it seems that Ferrari suddenly awakened to the fact that the family man might appreciate one of his masterpieces. After all, if Aston Martin and Maserati could build 2+2 cars so could he.

Left: The 250 GT Berlinetta Lusso – meaning luxury – was intended to be just that – luxurious gran turismo driving at its most opulent.

Bottom right: The 410 Superamerica was first seen in 1956 and was a short-lived attempt to capture the American styling mood of the period. Its successor, if it can be called that, was the 400 Superamerica shown as Superfast 11 in 1961. Below, The 400 lasted until 1964 before being discontinued.

Two prototypes were started on towards the end of March 1960 and one was used as the course car for the 1960 Le Mans event. Two production models were shown in the autumn, one at Paris and the other, a right-hand-drive car, at London. Both showed some new thinking on the styling from the prototypes. The fog lamps had disappeared and so had the louvers in the rear sail panels. The engine and gearbox had been moved forward to allow more interior space for the two additional rear seats. The tipo was designated 250 GT 2 + 2. It was a handsome car but unfortunately did not have a wide appeal and it was, of course, overshadowed by the 250 GT short wheelbase berlinetta. Around 900 250 GT 2 + 2s were built before their factory run came to an end in mid-1963.

At the Paris Salon in October 1962 a prototype of what was to become a classic Ferrari was introduced, designated the 250 GT berlinetta. The word Lusso (meaning luxurious or luxury) was added by the motoring press although not accepted by the works. The engine was still the Colombo-based 3-liter V12 set in a 2400mm wheelbase. A second prototype followed with coachwork, as usual, designed by Pinin Farina and built by Scaglietti. The ultimate design was a combination of two very good-looking cars, the front end bearing a similarity to the short wheelbase model and the rear following the lines of the 250 GTO with a slight 'spoiler' effect built into the rear end. The body was steel but the doors, hood and trunk lid aluminum. To give an easier ride the telescopic shock absorbers at the rear had concentric 'helper' springs and Watt linkage was employed (as on the GTO) for the rear axle's lateral location. Disk brakes were by now standard wear. The model probably had the best all-round vision up to that time with no quarter lights and the struts for the door, front and rear windshields gave minimal interference. All told 350 were built until production ceased in 1964.

Perhaps one of the surprising things about the Lusso is the fact that even today excellent used examples do not command a high price.

With the cessation of the Lusso's run so also ended the production of the under 3-liter front-engined V12 Ferraris. They had enjoyed a long innings and without doubt set up Ferrari in a strong financial position. They were fast and reliable cars which could be used either for grand touring or competition.

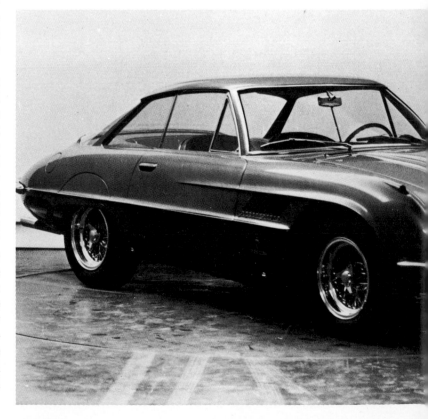

The V12 front-engined Gran Turismo cars over 3 liters

In the late summer of 1950 Ferrari announced a new model sports car, the type 340 America. This was the first car, other than the single seaters, to make use of the Lampredi 'long block' V12 engine. With a bore/stroke of 80×68mm the displacement was 4101cc.

By the following January, at the Brussels show, the chassis of a gran turismo car was on display and by the Turin show, in the spring, a complete model was available using the 4.1-liter unit of the 340 America. The tipo was known as the 342 America and it used similar equipment to the earlier car. It differed in the fact that the wheelbase was longer and the early models had a 5-speed gearbox in unit with the engine. The bodywork was a high-roof Touring coupe but some were similar in appearance to the 250 Europas and 375 Americas. Production was very limited.

By 1953 the 375 America was on view at the Paris Salon and shown at the same time as the 250 Europa, both cars sharing a common chassis. The V12 unit which powered the few cars which were built had a capacity of 4523cc and a power output of 300bhp at 6300rpm. Most of the coupes were designed and built by Pinin Farina.

As a replacement for the 375 America a chassis/engine of the next 'offering' was introduced at the 1955 Paris Salon to be followed by a complete car at Brussels early in 1956. This was the 410 Superamerica and the last of the line using the Lampredi 'long block' unit. Production was slow with about one car a month and few were built. A variety of bodies were used as Pinin Farina, Boano, Ghia and Scaglietti all had a hand in their production. The early cars were on a long wheelbase but by 1957 a shorter wheelbase model was introduced. The engine was all but 5-liters with a 4-speed gearbox in unit with the engine.

To replace the 410 Superamerica, Ferrari returned to a bored out and longer stroked version of the Colombo-based engine. Displacement was reduced to 3967cc. The new car was designated 400 Superamerica and on display at Brussels in January 1960.

Superfast was on show in Paris in 1956, a coupe design by Pinin Farina on the short wheelbase 410 Superamerica chassis. A wet-sump version of the 410 Sport 4.9-liter engine was used. It was notable for its cantilever-designed roof with no support pillars at the windshield and, following the American trend at that time, had rear end tail fins which did little to enhance its looks. The radiator grille was large and positioned low down.

An 'aerodynamic' coupe was on the stand at the 1960 Turin show. This was Superfast II and once more designed and built by Pinin Farina for his own use. The grille was small and elliptical and the headlamps retractable. A second version appeared a year later but with a larger grille and an airscoop on the bonnet. While the first car had fender skirts, these were not featured on the later car.

Based on the 1960 model and built on a 400 Superamerica chassis Superfast III was on view at Geneva in 1962. The air scoop from Superfast II was retained but a retractable grille cover was added and at the rear slender pillars were used.

Superfast IV also made its appearance in 1962 but changes had been carried out to the coachwork. The retractable headlamps were no longer in evidence and the rear wheel-arch covers had been removed.

The 1964 Geneva show saw the introduction of the handsome 500 Superfast, the only model in the series which went into limited production. Between 1964 and 1966 37 were built. The body was a Pinin Farina design showing some semblance to the earlier Superfast model. The 4963cc engine was based mainly on the Colombo unit and was new but used various components from the 330 GT 2+2. The early cars used a 4-speed gearbox with overdrive but later this unit was replaced by a 5-speed box which was also used by the later 330 GTs.

In 1963 Ferrari had the 330 GT 2+2 on the company's stand at the Paris Salon but clothed in a 250 GT 2+2 body. At the time it was known as the 330 America, an interim model of which only 50 were built. The 330 GT 2+2 Mk I with its own coachwork was at the 1964 Brussels show. It had four headlamps and its looks departed from the exotic designs the public expected from Ferrari. The V12 engine was Colombo-based with a capacity of 3967cc and a power output of 300bhp at 6600rpm. While it might not have looked Ferrari-like, it certainly behaved like one for it was extremely fast and very reliable and the back-seat passengers had more room than might have been expected in a 2 + 2. The early cars had a 4-speed gearbox and overdrive but later ones were equipped with a 5-speed box. After an initial production run of 625 the Mk II version was marketed. This model reverted to the normal, for those days, two headlamps and retained the 5-speed gearbox. The Mk II had a run of 460 when it went out of production in 1967.

While the 330 GT 2 + 2 was still coming from the factory one of the most handsome designs conceived by Pinin Farina was put on show at the Paris Salon in 1964. It was the 275 GTB and would be the last single overhead camshaft berlinetta built. It was also the first road-going Ferrari to have fully independent rear suspension. A spyder version, the 275 GTS, was also available using the same 3.3-liter power plant. Pinin Farina styled both bodies but the GTB was built by Scaglietti while the GTS was built by the designer. Pinin Farina's styling of the GTS was functional without being exotic, taking a leaf from his design of the 330 GT 2 + 2.

The buyer could, for the first time, have optional extras for the GTB – instead of three Weber 40 DCZ/6 or 40 DFI/1 carburetors, six Weber 40 DCF/6s could be fitted. Also for the first time on a gran turismo car Campagnolo alloy wheels were standard but the buyer could elect to have Borrani wires. The GTS had three Webers and Borranis and there were no options.

A second series GTB was shown at Frankfurt in 1965. As a cover for the carburetors there was a bulge on the bonnet, the vent wing on the driver's window was absent and there was more room for luggage. At the Paris Salon, only a month later, the front styling had been lengthened and such models are known as the 'long nosed' 275 GTB. The model seemingly underwent a number of changes during its life, some minor for styling purposes and some modifications to the engine. In 1966 at Paris a revized 275 GTB was introduced. For the first time each bank of cylinders had two overhead camshafts but in other respects the new dry-sump engine followed the earlier layout with a single plug, coil ignition and six Weber carburetors. The 5-speed gearbox was in unit with the differential. The revised car was designated 275 GTB/4.

The 275 GTBs showed clearly that when Ferrari produced the 250 GT berlinetta Lusso and the 330 GT 2 + 2, he was getting further away from the 'old style' GT models which were, in reality, thinly disguised racing cars with minimum creature comforts. The Lusso, the 330 and 275 GTB were more civilized cars and even the styling was getting away from the more functional (although still exotic) bodywork of the competition cars. Comfort and good rideability would be the norm for the gran turismo cars of the future.

To many Ferrarists the 330 GTC is the most civilized of the range of gran turismo models and the best road car. First shown at Geneva in March 1966 it used the 275 GTB chassis and the 4-liter engine of the 330 GT 2 + 2. As a styling exercise Pinin Farina decided on the front end of the 400 America, combining this with the rear end of the 275 GTS, and the result was an extremely handsome and elegant automobile. Although using the earlier 330's power unit the cylinder blocks had been redesigned as the GTC's 5-speed gearbox was mounted in unit with the differential. Suspension was, of course, all independent. As an optional extra air-conditioning could be installed. Some 600 models had been produced when it was taken out of production in 1968.

While the 330 GTC had been introduced in the spring of 1966 at Geneva a spyder model, the 330 GTS, came later in the year at the Paris autumn Salon. It was to be a replacement for the 275 GTS but after 100 or so examples had been built by Pinin Farina (who was also the designer) production ceased.

Alongside the 330 GTC at the Geneva show in 1966 Ferrari presented the last of what might be termed his large-

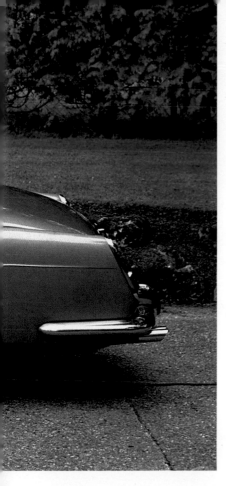

Left and below: Sometimes called the best road-going Ferrari ever built, the 330 GTC was introduced in 1965 with a body style which was a mixture of 500 Superfast at the front and 330 GT at the rear, and a four-liter V12 engine.

differential. Pinin Farina designed and built the 800 or so models, the last of which came from the factory in early 1971.

Ferrari was certainly keeping his expanding market going, for apart from the highly popular and saleable Dino 246 GT the larger models coming from the factory were filling a void which had not really been exploited – the exotic market.

A sensation was caused at the October 1968 Paris Salon when Enzo Ferrari uncovered a model which could rightly be called a legend even during the period of its production. Although it was designated Tipo 365 GTB/4 it was immediately dubbed the Daytona and is so called today. It was not only the most expensive Ferrari to come from the factory but for a number of years was the fastest road car ever built with a genuine 174mph tag!

The engine had twin overhead camshafts to each bank of cylinders with a capacity of 4.4-liters, a single plug per cylinder and coil ignition. Six Weber 40 DCN 20 carburetors fed the fuel and the power output was 320bhp at 7500rpm. There was dry sump lubrication and transmission was through a 5-speed gearbox in unit with the differential. Pinin Farina designed and built the prototype but Scaglietti was detailed to build the production models. Early cars had all the front lamps placed behind a full width wrap-around plastic cover but in mid-1971 paired retractable headlamps became standard. Although the model caused a sensation when it appeared there were those to whom the styling was not all that appealing with its long front end, a shortish driving compartment and Kamm-type rear end. However, the styling was functional and aggressive looking but it was somewhat heavy weighing in at 3600lbs.

A spyder version, the 365 GTS/4 was shown a year later at Frankfurt. A really beautiful design by Pinin Farina, it had been intended to build a very limited edition – only 15. The final figure was around 150. The design was so popular that many owners with the berlinetta have had the top removed, converting them to spyders.

The 365 GTC and GTS models were introduced in 1969 and were similar in many respects to the 330 GTC except that the engine was a 4.4-liter unit. Two years later a twin overhead camshaft model appeared but it had a short run with some 500 cars produced. Both were designed and built by Pinin Farina and from the experience of owners who tried both models most would agree that the single camshaft tipo was the better car. Both models, however, were in the range of the Ferrari luxury class. The cars were followed by another 2+2, the first for some time, designated 365 GT4. Using the same 4.4-liter engine with twin overhead camshafts it had the same power output of 320bhp and like its predecessor the rear suspension was equipped with hydro-pneumatic self-leveling. There were over 470 units built during a somewhat long lifespan from 1972 to 1976. This model was also in the luxury class.

With a number of elegant luxury models coming from the factory in quick succession, it seemed to the Ferrarist who was more interested in the road car evolved from the competition model that he might as well put behind him the old days. Manufacturers are not interested in the past. They have markets which have been researched and must plan their future models to fit them. While the engineer and coachwork designer are still important people in the world of the automobile they are certainly of less importance than the marketing men and auditors.

The ultimate shock to any die-hard came when the Paris Salon opened in October 1976. On the Ferrari stand was a

engined luxury cars. It was a spyder and designated 365 California. The V12 engine had a single camshaft per bank of cylinders and displaced 4390cc. There doesn't seem to have been any real point in its manufacture and after 14 models had been built the tipo was abandoned. Perhaps it was a preliminary run for the 365 GT 2+2 which appeared in 1967 at the Paris Salon. The same engine was used and the power output of 320bhp at 6600rpm was the same. However, the 5-speed gearbox was mated with the engine whereas the 365 California's gearbox was in unit with the

EUW 982V

Left: The Ferrari cockpit is almost certainly the object of more ambitions than any other make.

Below: The 1969 Dino 246 GTS which set a standard for Ferrari and others to aim at. The 2.4 liter V6 was mid-mounted in an excellently styled body.

model with automatic transmission – the 400 A – but there was also a manual version with a 5-speed gearbox. The 400 A was equipped with a 3-speed General Motors Turbo-Hydromatic automatic transmission. In many respects the new model was similar to the 365 GT4 2+2 but with the engine enlarged to 4823cc. Pinin Farina designed and still builds the cars which are the most luxurious so far to come from Ferrari.

The V12 engine displaced 4823cc and the rated power was 340bhp at 6500rpm. By mid-1979 carburetors had been replaced with Bosch K-Jetronic fuel injection reducing the power output to 310bhp at 6400rpm and a single Marelli distributor replaced the previous twin distributors. The limousine was now designated 400 GTi and 400ii Automatic. Included in the price was power steering and air conditioning. The interior was altered but not to any great extent but to give the whole a more up-market look. Perhaps one of the more significant alterations was to the rear suspension to give a smoother, more comfortable ride. Hydro-pneumatic self-leveling suspension has been incorporated, each piece of equipment working independently.

Whether any further refinements are carried out remains to be seen especially as the Ferrari-Pinin might be marketed in the not too distant future.

The V6 Gran Turismo cars

Up to 1957 Ferrari had built V12, in-line fours and in-line six cylinder cars but never a V6. In 1956 Vittorio Jano designed the first V6 unit and from that time a number of formula 1 and 2 cars had been produced with such a configuration.

Ferrari had never dabbled in formula 1 racing to any great extent although he had been highly successful with the formula in the early days – first with the 166 F2 V12 and then with the in-line four 500 F2. But he was to have a go in 1967 when the FIA would be bringing in new regulations for formula 2. These stipulated that the maximum displacement would be 1600cc unsupercharged and engines with up to six cylinders would be permitted. To help keep the cost of the cars to a reasonable figure the FIA also decreed that the engines used had to be from a production series with a minimum of 500 units built within a twelve-month period.

As with other manufacturers Ferrari must have been feeling the financial strain since he was involved not only in formula 1 but also in GT and prototype racing. Apart from this he was only building highly sophisticated and exotic cars and although they were produced in reasonable numbers high priced Ferraris were not an everyday saleable commodity!

Ferrari was in a bit of a dilemma as he certainly had no facilities for building 500 engines in a twelve-month period if he wanted to enter the formula 2 stakes. The problem was finally resolved when Fiat agreed to produce Ing Rocchi's V6 design although neither the independent Ferrari nor the non-racing Fiat factory were all that happy over the outcome of their talks. However, in the long run both were to benefit.

The run-up to the production Dino 206 GT were two sports prototypes – the 166 P and 206S. The first car was shown to the press and public at the Turin Show in 1967. While Pinin Farina designed the beautiful, sensual and flowing lines of the body he must have taken a hard look at

Drogo's design for the 166 P and the exquisite 206 S. Before deciding on the ultimate shape, Pinin Farina had produced several designs including one with gull-wings and front and rear spoilers.

The 65-degree V6 unit was placed transversely behind the driving compartment. The 1987cc engine had twin camshafts per bank of cylinders, a single plug, coil ignition and three Weber 40 DCF carburetors. The 5-speed gearbox was in unit with the differential. About 200 models were built by Scaglietti, all were berlinettas.

1969 was the year when Ferrari and Fiat joined forces and also the year when Ferrari put on show at Geneva his sensational Dino 246 GT which took the place of its smaller brother the 206 GT. The introduction of the model was probably Ferrari's answer to the smaller Porsche which was selling well and it was his intention to take a share of their market. The original price tag of £6000 made the car an attractive proposition, especially with the Ferrari connotation even if the badge on the nose and hub-caps proclaimed Dino and the script on the rear read Dino GT.

The 65-degree V12 engine was also placed transversely behind the driver's compartment. The engine was manufactured by Fiat and unlike Ferrari units whose block castings were silumin the 246 blocks were cast-iron. Bodies were built by Scaglietti and while the dimensions were larger, including the overall height, the shape of the coachwork was more voluptuous without the flatness of its predecessor. The only trouble was that instead of using aluminum Scaglietti used steel which helped to add an unwanted 400lbs and affected the overall performance although a maximum top speed of 150mph was probably justified. In spite of the extra weight the Dino 246 GT was an extremely handy and maneuverable car on the road with few vices. The main complaint of owners of the early cars was a certain shoddiness in the interior, poor quality carpeting, lack of attention to detail and poor fittings including the fittings of the bodywork panels, none of which was in the Ferrari tradition.

Three versions of the 246 were produced, the Type L (or Series I) with 357 examples built; the Type M (Series II) and with the introduction of the spyder, the Dino 246 GTS, in 1972 the Type E (Series III). This latter Type was introduced to comply with the stringent automobile legalities in force in the USA. The USA buyer also had a number of optional extras.

Overall there were probably in excess of 4000 models built and there can be no doubt that it was one of the best-selling cars the factory had designed even if many parts were of Fiat origin.

The 365 GTB/4 was produced by the works as a GT car, but this one has been privately converted to spyder bodywork, in which form it is possibly even more elegant.

The V8 Gran Turismo cars

The V8 configuration was not a new departure for Ferrari as in the early sixties such units had been used for both grand prix and sports racing cars. However, it was a new concept for a road-going automobile from the factory.

The first V8 gran turismo model was seen at the Paris Salon in the autumn of 1973 and was obviously to be the successor to the Dino 246 series. It was even designated Dino 308 GT4 2+2, which was a departure from Ferrari policy as it was thought that the appellation of Dino was exclusively for the V6 cars. Another surprise was the fact that Ferrari had, for once, after many years, turned to Bertone to design the coachwork. To many who had grown to love the lines of Pinin Farina's designs it was a bit of a shock. Somehow the exotic Ferrari had been turned into a rather plain looking car. It has to be admitted that attempting to give a 2+2 car flowing and sensuous lines has its difficulties especially when some headroom has to be found for the rear-seated passengers. So nobody should carp too much if the lines did not come up to what most expect from a Ferrari. Leaving out such criticism there can be no doubt that the performance and handling of the GT4 2+2 came up to expectations. While there might have been some sales resistance initially this has certainly been overcome since the model went out of production in 1980 as they are now sought after. Perhaps part of the resistance could be put down to the fact that using the name 'Dino' was an error on the part of Ferrari. In any case three years after its introduction the name and badges were changed to Ferrari.

To comply with modern Ferrari practice the 90 degree V8 twin overhead camshaft per bank of cylinders engine was located transversely behind the center line of the car. So that a low-profile could be achieved at the rear the 5-speed synchromesh gearbox was placed behind and not below the engine. Suspension, as with all Ferraris for many years, was fully independent, and to keep a smooth front line pop-up headlamps were incorporated. The 2926cc engine was rated at 250bhp at 7700rpm.

Two years later the second 308 was introduced. This was the berlinetta 308 GTB, first seen in Paris and the body could only have come from Pinin Farina. It really was a masterpiece of design and the fluting from the doors blended into the side panels and ended in a not too large air scoop aperture. A central all-round indent was carried round the body. Sail planes from the roof were taken to the rear opening of the engine lid and the rear end was a Kamm-type cut-off. Five-spoke Campagnolo wheels added to the attractive lines and a small front spoiler enhanced the appearance. The engine was basically similar to the 308 GT4 2+2 but with dry-sump lubrication. The power rating was given as 255bhp at 7600rpm and the top speed in excess of 150mph. The early cars were fiberglass but by mid-1977 the bodies were steel. All were and are built by Scaglietti. Also in 1977 the spyder or GTS version was shown at Frankfurt. It is always difficult to relate the word spyder to a berlinetta which has a portion of the roof removable so as to enjoy the 'passing' air — the term Targa would seem more appropriate. As with all cars with mid- or rear-mounted engines the question of baggage space arises. This is minimal, with some room under the hood but the main area is partitioned off behind the engine and while this might at first appear inadequate, quite a lot can be stowed away.

The overall performance is good all-round and was fit improved in 1981 when Bosch K-Jetronic fuel injection replaced the original four Weber 40 DCNF carburetors giving the 'new' car the designation 308 GTBi. Although the performance was good it was not good enough to out-perform some of the newer Porsches which, in turn, would mean a certain amount of sales resistance when a choice had to be made between the two marques. To improve this a four valve model was marketed in 1982 after the Mondial 8 had received the same treatment.

Above and below: The Pininfarina-styled Ferrari 365 GTC/4 – 'the hallmark of a man who has never accepted second best'.

By 1980 the 308 GT4 2 + 2 was replaced by the Mondial 8 using the same power plant as the 308 series but located transversely as for the GT4 behind the rear seats. To give more rear passenger space the wheelbase was lengthened and the roof was raised by five inches. To add to the general interior spaciousness the overall width was increased by three inches. Because four adults could now be accommodated the luggage area was enlarged so that it is now almost the same as that of the ordinary run-of-the-mill automobile.

Styling was left to Pinin Farina who did a far more satisfactory cosmetic job than Bertone, partly due to the greater overall length of the car. A small front spoiler gives an added refinement and the headlamps are naturally of the pop-up variety. During 1982 the two valve per cylinder head was changed to a four valve head and the engine received the same treatment as that of the 308 GTBi. Fiat or Ferrari changed the name by dropping the figure 8 and it became the Mondial quattrovalvole.

A number of changes have been made to the interior, the most notable being that made to the console over the central tunnel which now looks as though it has been designed into the car rather than placed in position as an afterthought. A number of detail changes have been carried out to instrumentation, and press buttons added, making for easier driving. The roof lining is a wool-type material which is fitted to the more expensive 512 BBi. Adjusting the outside mirrors has been made easier with the controls let into the driver's door and finally a Momo steering wheel has been included in the various improvements. The interior is, of course, upholstered in Connolly leather.

While there are still those who look back to the old days when a gran turismo was a thinly disguised racing car it has to be admitted that, under present day driving conditions, the current production models are built for and can be used as commuter cars. They can also be used as daily transport for other purposes – including shopping.

The Fiat 12 (Boxer) Gran Turismo cars

The Ferrari flat 12 or boxer engine goes back to the 1964/65 seasons when the 1.5-liter 512 F1 was practiced by Bandini before the 1964 Italian Grand Prix held over the Monza circuit. It was some years before the flat 12 unit was used in a production gran turismo car. The first inkling that such a model was in the offing was at the 1971 Turin Show but production did not start until 1973 when the first 365 GT4/BB rolled out of the factory gates.

The 4390cc engine was mounted at the rear and had twin overhead camshafts, a single plug, coil ignition and four Weber 40 IF3C carburetors. Pinin Farina designed the coachwork, Scaglietti built the main body parts of steel while the hood   doors and the rear deck engine cover were aluminum. The lower body panels were fiberglass and in contrast to the main body color were painted matt black. The styling was elegant and flowing, contrasting with the more aggressive appearance of the Daytona which it replaced.

In 1976 after a production run of nearly 390 units the model was replaced by the 512 BB. Some detail body changes were made to give the model its identity over its replacement. A narrow front spoiler was added and an air duct was included on the lower body panel ahead of the rear wheels and at the rear were four tail lamps instead of six.

The 512 BB (berlinetta boxer) has had many superlatives heaped upon it but in some respects its predecessor was its equal. The 512 BB had a power output of 340bhp at 6800rpm (the 365 GT4/BB was rated at 360bhp at 7500rpm). It would also seem that the 365 GT4/BB has been credited with a maximum speed of 181mph whereas the current 512 BB has an estimated top speed of 174mph which is no higher than that claimed for the Daytona. Agreed that speed is not the ultimate criteria of a car's performance for other important factors have to be considered, but it does

seem strange that what has been called a supercar can only muster the same speed as a car (the Daytona) which went out of production in 1973!

There can be no doubt that the current range of Ferrari road cars cannot be matched by any other manufacturer. And while Enzo Ferrari may have been over-cautious in the past the company which still carries his illustrious name, while still practising caution, is a market leader and will continue to be so for the foreseeable future.

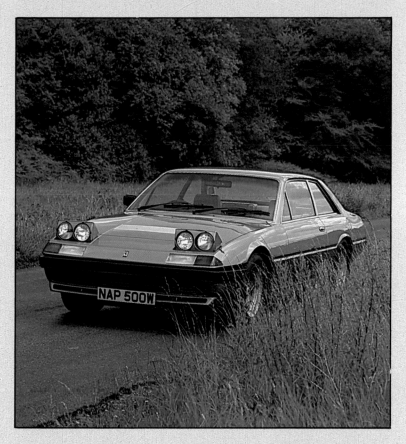

Above: It created something of a sensation when it appeared in 1976: the 400iA was not ony a saloon car, but was fitted with automatic transmission, something which was once anathema to sportscar manufacturers but is now accepted as the only sensible option in cars with this kind of power and performance.

250 SWB Berlinetta

Index

Page numbers in italics refer to illustrations.

Acknowledgment

The author and the publishers would like to thank Nick Georgano, Ann Charlish, Bridget Daly and Richard Nichols for their help in editing the book, David Eldred, who designed it, and Ronald Watson who compiled the index.

Special credit is due to Nicky Wright who took most of the photographs.

Thanks are due to the following who also supplied photographs:
Jeff Bloxham, pages 74, 54.
Geoffrey Goddard, pages 10, 14, 16, 18, 20, 22, 56, 58, 62, 66, 68, 70, 72, 74, 76, 78, 82.
Andrew Morland, pages 24, 30, 60.

We would also like to thank the following owners who kindly allowed their superb automobiles to be photographed for this book:
Richard Colton (250 LM Berlinetta)
David Cottingham (340 MM)
Chris Drake (750 Monza)
J H & T C Harrison (1957 250 Testa Rossa)
Paul Jackman (1948 TIPO 166 Corsa Spyder)
Mrs W A Lockley-Cook (1972 365 GTB/4)
Maranello Engineering (DINO 246 GT Spyder)
Nick Mason (DINO 206 SP)
Dudley Mason-Styrron (DINO Tasman F2)
Modena Engineering (512 BB Berlinetta Boxer; 365 CTC/4; Type 410 Super America; 275 GTB; 250 GT Berlinetta Lusso; 1981 400 Automatic; 330 GTC; 1982 308 GTS
Don Nelson (250 LM Berlinetta; 1962 250 GTO LM)
R A Parker (275 GTB)
Roy Pearce (1982 S12 BB Berlinetta Boxer; 365 Daytona GTB/4 Spyder)
Peter Sugden (250 SWB Berlinetta)